The Promise, The Presence, And The Power of The Holy Spirit

James E. Puckett Sr.

© 2023 James E. Puckett Sr.

All rights reserved.

Dedication

I dedicate this book to anyone who dares to accept the Promise of the Holy Spirit, acknowledge the Presence of the Holy Spirit, and receive the Power of the Holy Spirit.

TABLE OF CONTENTS

Introduction 1

Author's Reflections 4

Chapter 1 The Promise of the Holy Spirit 18

Chapter 2 The Presence and Power of the Holy Spirit 47

Chapter 3 Why Should Believers be Baptized with the Holy Spirit? 96

Chapter 4 Do Not Be Ignorant about Tongues 103

Conclusion 115

Introduction

Has anyone ever promised you something? Something that you've always wanted or hoped for? Something you've dreamed about doing or having in your life? Especially if it was something that you yearned for? Something you've one day been expecting. I'm talking about the things you've always been excited to have as your own or call yours. I know I have—both as a child and as an adult.

When I was a little boy, I recall wishing and hoping for a specific toy for Christmas, my birthday, or some other special occasion. That's when my expectation would explode with utmost joy and hope. My parents wouldn't even need to promise me that they would get it, but just say that they would try.

I never expected them to make any promises because I knew they might be unable to keep them. Not because they didn't want or desire to, but because I knew they probably couldn't afford it. But knowing they would try was enough for me. It was enough to keep me lit up with hope, joy, and excitement. Likewise, if you're a parent and promised your children something that they had dreamed about most of their life and wanted badly, you witness the joy and hope in their voices and on their faces. The glimmer in their eyes and the positivity in their actions would surprise you. And as a parent, you would work hard to keep that promise to the extent of your ability.

Maybe you had similar experiences as a child. Maybe you wanted and hoped for that special something, and your parents promised that they would do their best to get it for you. But now that you're all grown up, I want to ask you these questions:

(1) Do you still get excited about promises today?

(2) Do you look forward to promises made toward you today as you did when you were a child?

(3) Or do you just let promises pass through one ear and out the other since most of the promises that were made to you have gone unfilled?

As an adult, you may look at promises as something that might happen or might not. As an adult, we probably wouldn't put as much hope in a promise made by our parents as we did when we were children (if you still have a living parent). I say this because we are now depending on another adult. As a child, we put a lot more trust in our parents than we do after growing up. I'm not suggesting that we shouldn't put our trust in our parents. Neither am I saying that we shouldn't put our trust in man. But we know that man's promises are not always yea and amen like God's promises. This is what the Bible says about God's promises:

> For all the promises of God in him are yea, and in him Amen, unto the glory of God by us
> (2 Corinthians 1:20).

Man has flaws and circumstances that are subject to change. There is no such changing with God. Therefore, there is no change in His promises. Jesus is the same yesterday, today, and forever (Hebrews 13:8). Romans 3:4 says,

> God forbid: yea, let God be true, but every man a liar; as it is written, That thou mightest be justified in thy sayings, and mightest overcome when thou art judged.

We also see that the latter part of James 1:17 says, "He does not change and he makes no shadow by turning." The point is that what God has promised, He is able to bring to pass.

I want to clear the air of one other thing before we go any further: being baptized with the Holy Spirit does not guarantee, for a believer, a life of no pain, sickness, or trouble. We know that this world we live in is not free of these things. Being baptized with the Holy Spirit does not mean believers will have a trouble-free life.

Author's Reflections

Now, all of us must understand that we were created for a higher purpose. God has destined all of us for something great, and we should be in constant pursuit of that higher purpose. Your peace, your joy, your expectations, and your prosperity are all tied to it. When God created us, the Bible says He breathed into our nostrils the breath of life, and we became living souls (Genesis 2:7). The word "breath" is the Spirit of God. Therefore, the Spirit of God was released inside us when He breathed into our nostrils, filling our lungs with air, and giving us this beautiful life. That was the purpose of the Spirit of God, not only at your creation, but also after we receive Jesus as our Lord and Savior. The Holy Spirit lives inside all of us. The Holy Spirit doesn't just want to live in us; He wants to be an active part of our lives in a positive way. Look at Romans:

> But you do not live in the flesh. You live in the Spirit, assuming, of course, that the Spirit of God lives inside of you. The truth is that anyone who does not have the Spirit of the Anointed living within does not belong to God (Romans 8:9, Voice Translation).

The above verse tells us that born-again people are not ruled by their flesh but rather by the Spirit of God that took up residence in them at the new birth. But there is another infilling that is available after the new birth: the baptism of the Holy Spirit. This baptism could be called "the Baptism of Power." I like to think of it as a higher gear when life seems to be an uphill battle, and I need extra power to make it to the top. Being baptized with the Holy Spirit means I have a reserve of the supernatural living inside of me that's ready to produce power and drive me through the struggles and challenges of life.

You and I will never be our best or feel absolute fulfillment in Christ until we connect with what God has intended for our lives. The Holy Spirit is one of those connections. Many of the problems and frustrations people are experiencing in life are because they aren't walking in the divine purpose that God has for their life. This is why so many people are guilty of blaming others for their condition and misfortune. They blame their family, their upbringing, and the world's system for their failures in life.

But I believe that there comes a time in all our lives when each of us must take responsibility and say, "There must be something better." Maybe you're reading this book, and something has happened in your life that changes everything for the better, regardless of what is going on! Regardless of the mistakes of your past! Regardless of your misfortunes.

There is so much more promised to you. For example, Ephesians 3:20 says, "Now unto him, that is able to do exceeding abundantly above all that we ask or think, according to the power that worketh in us." In 1 John 4:4, Scripture also says, "Ye are of God, little children, and have overcome them: because greater is he that is in you than he that is in the world." The Greater One mentioned there is the Holy Spirit.

The phrase "Holy Spirit" is used in the New Testament as "Spirit" and "Ghost," meaning the same word, "*pneuma,*" or air. It's important to note that while the word "Spirit" is used alone, the word "Ghost" is always preceded by the word "Holy." According to *Webster's American Dictionary of the English Language, 1828 Edition*, the word "holy" means properly, whole, entire, or perfect in a moral sense. Additionally, according to *Vine's Complete Expository Dictionary of Old and New Testament Words*, the word "spirit" means pneuma, which indicates wind. It also means to breathe or blow. Likewise, the word "holy" from Vine's Dictionary signifies pure and devoted and something or someone. So, the Holy Spirit or the Holy Ghost is the whole, entire, and perfect Spirit that Jesus will breathe upon His children who are baptized in the Holy Spirit (Luke 3:16).

The Bible has "types," or metaphors, of the Holy Spirit. The five types I would like to emphasize are:

1. Wind (John 3:8, John 20:20, Acts 2:2, and Romans 8:16).
2. Water (Isaiah 44, John 4:14, John 7:37-39, and 1 Corinthians 12:13).
3. Oil (1 Samuel 16:13, Isaiah 61:1, and Acts 10:38).
4. Dove (Matthew 3:16, Mark 1:10, and Luke 3:22).
5. Fire (Matthew 3:11 and Acts 2:3-4).

You will see me reference many of these and other Scriptures more than once throughout this book to help support my message. Let the Word be established or confirmed by two or more witnesses (Matthew 18:16).

I chose the title of this book, *The Promise, The Presence, and The Power of the Holy Spirit*, because I wanted to highlight the Holy Spirit in His truest form. If you have accepted Jesus as your Lord and Savior, then the Holy Spirit lives inside of you. Jesus said,

> And I will pray the Father, and he shall give you another Comforter, that he may abide with you forever; (John 14:16).

The Comforter that Jesus was speaking of is truly the Holy Spirit that every person has been promised. This promise can be seen operating in power throughout the New Testament. In the book of Acts, Chapter 1, the early church received the *promise* of the Holy Spirit. In Acts 2, the early church witnessed the *presence* of the Holy Spirit, and in Acts 3, the early church experienced the *power* of the Holy Spirit. Let's take a look:

> And, being assembled together with them, commanded them that they should not depart from Jerusalem, but wait for the promise of the Father, which, saith he, ye have heard of me. For John truly baptized with water; but ye shall be baptized with the Holy Ghost not many days hence (Acts 1:4-5).

> Picture yourself among the disciples: A sound roars from the sky without warning, the roar of a violent wind, and the whole house where you are gathered reverberates with the sound (Acts 2:2, Voice Translation).

So, we can see the *promise* of the Holy Spirit being fulfilled in Acts 1, and the *presence* of Him in Acts 2. I intentionally left out a reference for the *power* because I will go deeper into those details later in the book. Furthermore, after they were baptized with the Holy Spirit, there would be power released that would cause them to be a witness for Him (Acts 1:8). The same baptism that these men experienced is here for all of us today.

In this book, I will focus my attention on the first three chapters of Acts, other books of the Bible, as well as my own personal life experiences to help convey my message. I will give most of my attention to the Power of the Holy Spirit. Not that the Promise and Presence aren't important, but when the Promise and Presence are fulfilled, the Power is released.

I chose the book of Acts to begin my research for this book, because this is where we find the Holy Spirit operating in power throughout the church. The book of Acts and the Gospels show the working relationship between man and the Holy Spirit. It was the power of the Holy Spirit in Jesus' life that gave Him the power to preach about the kingdom of God, heal the sick, cast out demons, and set captives free (Luke 4:14-19; Matt. 4:23). We will see that the same power in Acts 2 gave the disciples authority. Jesus is the model of a Sprit-filled, Spirit-entitled life.

This power is produced by the working presence of the Holy Spirit. Let me give you an example. When you and I are promised something, and that promise is carried out toward us, we express excitement and an overwhelming, joyful reaction. It is promised, it shows up (presence), and then there is rejoicing (power).

Likewise, when the promise and presence of the Holy Spirit are manifested into our lives, there is excitement, joy, and fulfillment produced by His power. This is similar to what happened in the Upper Room on the day of Pentecost. The Bible says there was a rushing, mighty wind that filled the entire house where they were gathered (Acts 2:2).

Remember, the rushing wind is also a type of the Holy Spirit. The Holy Spirit not only filled the house but also filled every person in the house. The wind was power produced by the Holy Spirit. The wind was the Holy Spirit. How could these men be in the house and not be filled with the same substance that the house was filled with? I don't think they held their breath until the wind of the Spirit stopped blowing. No, they were filled too.

While we discuss the promise, presence, and power of the Holy Spirit from the New Testament, I want you to be aware that there are many Scriptures that prove that the Holy Spirit was present and working in the Old Testament as well.

In the Old Testament, the phrase "Holy Spirit" is only recorded three times, but throughout Old Testament Scriptures, it is evident that the Holy Spirit was at work. The Holy Spirit was at work from Genesis to Revelation, but after Jesus went to be with the Father, He came in a different manifestation. The Bible says that the Spirit of God was responsible for forming the earth in the beginning (Genesis 1:1-2).

The Bible also tells us about the working of the Word in the beginning. In John, we read:

> In the beginning was the Word, and the Word was with God, and the Word was God. The same was in the beginning with God. All things were made by him; and without him was not anything made that was made (John 1:1-3).

According to the verse above, the Word was involved in the creation of the world. Remember, Jesus was the Word made flesh and made to dwell amongst us (John 1:14). Since the Word was with God during creation, and Jesus is the Word made flesh, then Jesus was also there with God during the creation of the world as we know it. Not in flesh and bones, but in Spirit. God and Jesus have been working in partnership since the beginning of time. Furthermore, since the Holy Spirit came from the Father, then He was there with Jesus and the Father at the beginning of creation too. The Father, The Son, and The Holy Spirit are three expressions of one person.

In the Old Testament, the Holy Spirit *came upon* and *departed* from the people who spoke for God. We can see this in Ezekiel 2:2 with the prophet Ezekiel; in Judges 3:10 with Othniel; in Judges 6:34 with Gideon; in Judges 13:25 and 14:6 with Samson; and in 1 Samuel 10:9 -10 with Saul. As a side note, I also want to point out that the Holy Spirit left Saul because of his disobedience (1 Samuel 16:14).

We can see from the Scriptures above that the Holy Spirit came upon *and* departed from the people who spoke for God in the Old Testament. These people were not baptized with the Holy Spirit. Remember, Jesus had not been born yet. Unlike the Old Testament, the baptism I'm speaking of is the One that lives inside of you and me, and when baptized with Him, we receive a supernatural power from Him when He comes upon us. Look at Acts:

> But ye shall receive power after the Holy Ghost is come upon you; and ye shall be witnesses unto Me both in Jerusalem, and in all Judea and in Samaria, and unto the uttermost part of the earth (Acts 1:8).

There is a phrase from the verse above I want to explore just a bit. That phrase is, "after the Holy Ghost is come upon you." When I hear this phrase, I have a vision of a bee or yellow jacket landing on me and stinging me. That happened to me several times when I was a small child. The sting that they produce causes a person to move under the power that it had produced. I'm not suggesting that being filled with the Holy Spirit is harmful in any way; I'm just emphasizing the fact that He produces power when He comes upon you, like being stung by one of those powerful insects. The sting of those insects will cause a person to do things they thought they would never do. Likewise, when the Holy Spirit comes upon a believer, he is endowed with the power to do things he could otherwise not do.

Even though these disciples were believers and had the Holy Spirit living inside them, they were promised a power that would give them the ability to be an institutor of Christ's kingdom. However, the power would only come *after* the Holy Ghost came upon them. The power was not there until the Holy Spirit came. This means that before that moment, they did *not* possess the power to carry out the works of God. After they were baptized with the Holy Spirit, He would take control during their spiritual activities and cause them to do the work of the Father. He would take the natural and turn it into the supernatural.

This is important to understand as we move forward because as New Testament Christians, it's important to know that you and I cannot operate in the power of God and do the work He has commanded us to do until we are filled or baptized with the Holy Spirit. It is a spiritual and moral power. This power is produced by the dynamism of the Holy Ghost sent from the Father.

In the book of Acts, we will see people filled with the Holy Spirit (Acts 2:4; 9:17), people receive the Holy Spirit (Acts 8:17), the Holy Spirit fall upon people (Acts 10:44), the Holy Spirit be poured out on people (Acts 10:45), and the

Holy Spirit come upon people (Acts 19:6). These are the fulfillments of the promise made by Jesus that the church would be baptized with the Holy Spirit (Acts 1:5).

It is no different for the believers of today. When believers are baptized with the Holy Spirit, they are candidates for a supernatural power to rise *within* them through the Holy Spirit. The Holy Spirit lives inside them forever, but He comes upon them and provides a supernatural power to do the work of the kingdom. To experience this supernatural power, the Holy Spirit must be given *free will* in the life of the believer, and the atmosphere must be right. Therefore, we cannot avoid or ignore the Holy Spirit. We, as believers, must create a welcome setting and invite Him into our world. The Bible tells believers not to grieve the Holy Ghost (Ephesians 4:30), so it's imperative that we allow Him to have a free course in our life.

In the book of Joel, we see that the prophet Joel forecasted that there would be a supernatural force available to every believer. I want you to know that if you are reading this and have yet to experience the infilling of the Holy Spirit, it's available to you. At the end of this book, you will have an opportunity to receive His baptism. Let's look at what Joel told us:

> Then it will come about at a later time that I will pour out my Spirit on every person. Your sons and your daughters will prophesy. Your elderly people will dream dreams, and your young people will see visions. Also, at that time I will pour out my Spirit upon men and women servants (Joel 2:28-29, International Standard Version).

Even though the term "Spirit" is used in these verses, it is a direct reference to the Holy Spirit being poured out. It's the same Holy Spirit that Jesus said the Father would send after He ascended to the Father. This is the Spirit that would dwell in every believer. John says:

> Even the Spirit of truth; whom the world cannot receive, because it seeth him not, neither knoweth him: but ye know him; for he dwelleth with you, and shall be in you. I will not leave you comfortless: I will come to you (John 14:17-18).

Jesus stated that the world cannot receive or know the Holy Spirit. Unbelievers or people living as the world lives cannot receive Him and don't know Him. In fact, the only way to know and receive the Holy Spirit is by knowing and receiving the Son of God, Jesus Christ. You *must* be born again (John 3:3). The Holy Spirit only lives inside those who have made Jesus the Lord and Savior of their life. He is there to comfort us in all circumstances, whether good or bad. You might ask, "Why didn't Jesus stay on Earth as a man?" Well, here's the answer: Jesus could not stay on earth as a man *and* be in the will of the Father. His reason for being born, dying on the cross, being buried, and rising from the dead was to fulfill the Will of the Father. The Father's Will was to give the New Testament Church a better promise. The Father's desire was to grant His people a redemption plan that would be everlasting and unchanging.

Some might say, "Well, I would rather have Jesus Himself stay here! It would be better for us all if He had remained here on Earth! That way I would be able to touch Him. I would be able to see Him. And most importantly, I would be able to talk to Him." Others might argue, "Well, if Jesus cared anything about me, He wouldn't have left Earth".

I certainly understand why you may feel this way. But to tell you the truth, Jesus is not returning to Earth to be with us in the form of a human. No matter how much we wish, hope, or pray, Jesus is not coming back to Earth in that way. You might say, "I am using my faith for Jesus to come back as a human to live and be with me on Earth." All I can tell you is that you are operating in blind faith. It will never happen. Look at the evidence found in Romans 10:6-7:

> But this is what the Scriptures say about being made right through faith: "Don't say to yourself, 'Who will go up into heaven?'" (This means "Who will go up to heaven to get Christ and bring him down to earth?") "And don't say, 'Who will go down into the world below?'" (This means "Who will go down to get Christ and bring him up from death?") (Romans 10:6-7, Easy-to-Read Version).

The Scriptures above tell us that believers shouldn't say anything about bringing Jesus back to Earth or back from the dead. First, He is not dead, but forever alive. Secondly, it was never the plan or purpose of the Father to have Him return to Earth in that image. Jesus said that He would send the Holy Spirit after He was gone to the Father. We as believers must believe Him by faith. We cannot live our lives hoping, wishing, or praying for Jesus to come back to Earth in the form of a human being. By faith, believers must learn to accept that the Holy Spirit was sent by the Father in the absence of His Son, Jesus. The promise and the coming of the Holy Spirit is better for all of us here on Earth. Jesus said it Himself:

Nevertheless, I tell you the truth; It is expedient for you that I go away: for if I go not away, the Comforter will not come unto you; but if I depart, I will send him unto you (John 16:7).

When we accept Jesus Christ as our Lord and Savior, we receive a power that can change any negative thing that we go through. That power comes from being baptized with the Holy Spirit. When Jesus said in John 16:7 that if He didn't go away, the Comforter would not come, He was speaking of the infilling of the Holy Spirit. We receive the Holy Spirit at the new birth, but when we are filled with or baptized with the Holy Spirit, it is the promise of this infilling of power that He was speaking of.

Jesus Himself confessed that the promise of the Holy Spirit was much better than Him being there in the flesh. You may ask, "Why?" Well, if Jesus didn't go to the Father but instead remained here as a man, it would be impossible for Him to be omnipresent with us. Some people may find the above verse depressing. It's not meant to depress us, but rather to excite us and give us joy and renewed hope. While He no longer walks beside us physically, He is always with us spiritually. To me, this is a much better deal.

Because Jesus departed to the Father, I have power available to me as well as around-the-clock access to Him. He is never busy or preoccupied. The same is true for you if you have made Jesus your Lord and Savior and received the infilling or baptism of the Holy Spirit. Again, I don't want to confuse anyone. If you are born again, the Holy Spirit lives inside you. What I am presenting in this book is another attribute or characteristic of the Holy Spirit—the *power* to produce miracles, signs, and wonders. Jesus, Himself had to be baptized with the Holy Spirit. Let's look at Luke:

> Now when all the people were baptized, it came to pass, that Jesus also being baptized, and praying, the heaven was opened, And the Holy Ghost descended in a bodily shape like a dove upon him, and a voice came from heaven, which said, Thou art my beloved Son; in thee I am well pleased (Luke 3:21-22).

After showing Himself to His disciples on the day of His resurrection, one of the things Jesus did was to fill them with the Holy Spirit. Remember, these were the disciples of Jesus. The very men that had been with Him during His earthly ministry. Jesus understood that because He could no longer be with them on Earth, they needed to be filled with the Holy Spirit to be fulfilled.

> He breathed on them, and said unto them, Receive the Holy Spirit (John 20:22).

Jesus knew that just being with Him wouldn't be enough to fulfill the commission He would charge them with (Mark 16:15). Jesus knew that without the infilling of the Holy Spirit, they wouldn't have the ability to do the greater works (John 14:12). I believe the following verse explains some of the greater works:

> And when he is come, he will reprove the world of sin, and of righteousness, and of judgment: Of sin, because they believe not on me; Of righteousness, because I go to my Father, and ye see me no more; Of judgment, because the prince of this world is judged (John 16:8-11).

He is the Judge and Jury of our life and of Satan himself. However, He is not only the Judge and Jury but also our Guide into all truths.

A few notes before we move forward. As we have already explained, the Bible refers to the "Helper" I'm talking about as "the Holy Ghost" and "the Holy Spirit." In the remainder of this book, I will reference Him as the Holy Spirit. Just know that the Holy Ghost and Holy Spirit are one and the same.

Also, I would like to make it clear up front that I do not, by any means, claim to know everything about the Holy Spirit. I'm still learning about and growing in the things of God, as should be the goal for every Christian. So, I'll be the first to tell you that what you read about the Holy Spirit in this book is not all that could be said about Him.

All I can share with you is what I have learned from the Bible about Him and my personal experiences with Him. Anything else would be hearsay and not fair to my readers or to the Word of God. Please forgive me if I have overlooked something or failed to share something that you might know about the Holy Spirit. Again, I'm sharing with you my personal experiences and the knowledge I have gained from the Scriptures about the Holy Spirit.

Chapter 1

The Promise of the Holy Spirit

> For all the promises of God in him are yea, and in him Amen, unto the glory of God by us (2 Corinthians 1:20).

I shared this verse earlier, but let's take a deeper look into it. It tells us that all of God's promises are His last *Will* to the church. This *Will* is His Word and what He has said is always final. The promise that all His promises are final is one that we can trust and find hope in. We don't have to wonder or guess what God will do. Everything He has said in His Word is exactly what He will do. All His promises have already been granted to us and are waiting for us to enjoy. All we have to do is position ourselves where we can receive them. The Holy Spirit assists us in getting in that position.

Now that I am no longer a child but an adult, I still get excited about promises toward me. But now that I'm all grown up, I don't value people's promises as final. And you shouldn't either. You have probably been promised something in your lifetime. It could have been a promise from your boss at work—the promise of a raise or a position that you always wanted. It could also have been a promise from a relative or close friend. Nevertheless, it probably got your hopes high and brought a sense of joy to you. But many times, these promises were not carried out or fulfilled for one reason or another. Even though we are no longer children, we can still place a measure of hope in the promises made to us. We should just make sure that we qualify where the promises come from.

But the promise I want to explore in this book is the Promise of the Holy Spirit and what follows—His Presence and His Power. The Holy Spirit wants to present Himself to you and produce power in your life. All the promises in the Holy Scriptures are final, even if we fail to receive them. Once again, I want to share James 1:17,

> Every good gift and every perfect gift is from above, and cometh down from the Father of lights, with whom is no variableness, neither shadow of turning.

The Passion Translation says it like this:

> Every gift God freely gives us is good and perfect, streaming down from the Father of lights, who shines from the heavens with no hidden shadow or darkness and is never subject to change.

What the above verses are really saying is this: *Every promise we find in the Holy Scriptures is given by God, and whatever happens in our lives, and no matter the circumstances, He will never change His mind.* From Genesis to Revelation, the Bible is full of the promises made by God. But let me be clear about one thing; neither you nor I can bring these promises to pass on our own, even though God has promised them to us. We must factor God into the equation in every area of our life. The promise I will explore in this book is the Promise of the Holy Spirit as well as the two main functions of His acts: His Presence and His Power.

There are many promises in the Holy Scriptures. In my opinion, the greatest promise of all is the Promise of the

Holy Spirit. Jesus spoke many things and made many promises to His disciples before He departed to the Father. One of the things He promised was the sending of the Holy Spirit. These men were to be baptized with this promise, which was the Holy Spirit. And after being baptized, they would speak in other tongues and receive Power, which we will discuss in more detail later. In my opinion, there are only two other elements that are more powerful than the Holy Spirit. One is the Word of God Himself, and the other is the blood of Jesus.

This is what the Bible has to say about the power of the Word of God.

> For the word of God is quick, and powerful, and sharper than any twoedged sword, piercing even to the dividing asunder of soul and spirit, and of the joints and marrow, and is a discerner of the thoughts and intents of the heart (Hebrews 4:12).

Furthermore, we must realize that without the shedding of the blood of Jesus, you and I would be responsible for our sins. However, because Jesus shed His blood on the cross, every person can be remitted of his or her sins. So, we can see that all three: the Holy Spirit, the Word of God, and the blood of Jesus are promises from God the Father, to whosoever will believe and receive Him. And they all have their special place in the life of a Christian. Please don't hear me say that the Holy Spirit is more powerful than the Word of God or the blood of Jesus.

Martyn Lloyd-Jones said this: "Nothing is more dangerous than to put a wedge between the Word and the Spirit, to emphasize either one at the expense of the other. It is the

Spirit and the Word, the Spirit upon the Word, and the Spirit in us as we read the Word."

God knew that His children would need supernatural power after Jesus left Earth to join Him in Heaven. The Father knew that we would have to contend with principalities, powers, and rulers of the darkness of this age and defend ourselves against spiritual hosts of wickedness in the heavenly places. The only way we can stand strong is by putting on the whole armor of God (Ephesians 6:12). Therefore, He gave us the Holy Spirit as a Defender, which is more powerful than anything you or I will face in life (1 John 4:4).

The Bible tells us that the Holy Spirit is the third person of the Christian Godhead. We, as Christians, refer to the Trinity as containing three persons—the Father, the Son, and the Holy Spirit. The Bible lets us know that these three are one (1 John 5:7). All three agree. However, to keep in context with my subject, we'll gear our attention to the Power of the Holy Spirit.

Each morning when my feet hit the floor, I confess these words:

> Good morning, Father God. Good morning, Jesus Christ, Good morning, Holy Spirit. This is your son, reporting for duty. Whatever it is you want me to do today, I am willing and able. I am willing because I have decided to serve you unconditionally. I am able, because I can do all things through Christ *who* strengthens me.

I must emphasis the need to acknowledge all three Persons of the Trinity before I start my day. I have come to realize that because They work in unity with each other, it is important to have a relationship with all three.

The Trinity is one person expressed in three ways: The Father, The Son, and the Holy Spirit. The Son is the Word made flesh, and the Holy Spirit is the demonstrated works of the Father.

I want to briefly mention one other detail. I have heard some people refer to the Holy Spirit as "*it*" The Holy Spirit is not considered an "it." He is the third *person* of the Godhead. Hence, we will use the pronouns He or Him throughout this book, when appropriate, to identify the Holy Spirit.

When I first began to learn about the Holy Spirit, it was difficult for me to grasp how the Holy Spirit could be the third *person* of the Godhead and, at the same time, have a distinctive role outside of the three. Then, I remembered someone saying that I should view the Holy Spirit as a person, just as we view the Father and Jesus as people. The Father and Jesus are the same when it comes to functions, but they have different personalities. The Father, Jesus, and the Holy Spirit are One, but each function differently because of their personality. I guess you could say that each one of them has a different role to play in our lives.

After I started to think of the Holy Spirit as a person, I began to understand how they could be one but have different functions. So, view the Holy Spirit as a person and that His personality is unique from that of the Father and Jesus. Look at Matthew:

> And whosoever speaketh a word against the Son of man, it shall be forgiven him: but whosoever speaketh against the Holy Ghost, it shall not be

forgiven him, neither in this world, neither in the world to come (Matthew 12:32).

Do you see the unique difference between Jesus and the Holy Spirit? I would not advise it, but evidently, you can say things about Jesus and still be in good standing with the Father, but not about the Holy Spirit. Even though the Holy Spirit and Jesus have different personalities, they are both manifested from the Father Himself and work in unity to do the *Will* of the Father. They are never in conflict with each other.

The Holy Spirit is the One that inspired the prophets to write the Holy Scriptures, and then it was Him that illuminated them to the church. Therefore, the Word of God, Jesus, and the Holy Spirit are inseparable. That is the reason why the three are called the Trinity, the Godhead consisting of three persons—Father, Son, and Holy Spirit. The Father is the head of the Godhead. Jesus Himself was the Holy Spirit when He walked the Earth. I like to think that the Holy Spirit is the communicated power of the Trinity. Look at John:

> And the Word was made flesh, and dwelt among us, (and we beheld his glory, the glory as of the only begotten of the Father,) full of grace and truth (John 1:14).

I don't want anyone to misunderstand me when I said, "the Holy Spirit is the communicated power of the Trinity." All three people of the Godhead have equal power, and each one agrees with the workings of the others. Other than the promise of Jesus as our Savior, in my opinion, the Promise of the Holy Spirit is the greatest promise made by God throughout the entire Bible, and Christians can look forward to it in this lifetime. All the other promises in the Bible hinge on Him.

Someone might say, "But didn't the promise of the Holy Spirit manifest on the day of Pentecost?" The answer is yes. But not every Christian has received Him in that way. There are many Christians who have yet to receive the infilling or baptism of the Holy Spirit with the evidence of speaking in other tongues. This is a promise of always having, in our presence, every word that Jesus has spoken and the ability for Him to speak to us at any given time. The promise of a Comforter, Counselor, Helper, Intercessor, Advocate, Strengthener, Spirit of Truth, Teacher, Mind Regulator, Standby, Paraclete, and more. All these are characteristics that illustrate His power, which you and I are entitled to when we receive Him.

> But the Comforter, which is the Holy Ghost, whom the Father will send in my name, he shall teach you all things, and bring all things to your remembrance, whatsoever I have said unto you (John 14:26).

On the day Jesus was taken up into Heaven, He instructed His disciples to wait in the Upper Room at Jerusalem for the promise which they had been hearing about. That promise was the Promise of the Holy Spirit.

> But when the Comforter is come, whom I will send unto you from the Father, even the Spirit of truth, which proceedeth from the Father, he shall testify of me: And ye also shall bear witness, because ye have been with me from the beginning (John 15:26-27).

> And, being assembled together with them, commanded them that they should not depart from

Jerusalem, but wait for the promise of the Father, which, saith he, ye have heard of me (Acts 1:4).

Notice from John 15:26 that Jesus said that the Holy Spirit shall testify of Him. After we are baptized with the Holy Spirit, we are now the witnesses of Christ. Our job is to tell the world about Jesus through the knowledge of the Holy Spirit. When reading the Bible and praying, it is through the Holy Spirit that we receive the knowledge of Jesus and are able to testify of Him. There are things about Jesus that we don't know, but the Father desires for us to know them. If we can't get it from the Word of God, it is revealed to us through the Holy Spirit if He so chooses.

One thing I want to make clear before we go any further. That is, if you have received the new birth and have been born again but have not been baptized with the Holy Spirit with the evidence of speaking in other tongues, that doesn't mean that you aren't capable of hearing from God or witnessing for Jesus. Nor am I saying that you will not go to Heaven. But what I do know from my own personal experiences, which I will share later in the book, is that everything spiritual about my life changed after I was baptized with the Holy Spirit and started to speak in other tongues.

I heard someone explain it like this: "A believer without the baptism of the Holy Spirit is like a car without a passing gear." They're just living life with no additional power when they need help or direction. The Holy Spirit is the believer's extra gear that produces the power needed for living a faith-filled and victorious life.

Obedience to God is Necessary to Receive the Promise

Jesus announced that the Promise was to be sent by the Father. God's plan has always been to redeem man back into good standing with Him. We can see this with Noah and the flood and, later, with Adam in the garden. His redemptive plan for you and me was through His son, Jesus. The Law alone was not sufficient for man's behavior. Even though God did not do away with the Law (Matthew 5:17), He did replace the Law with a better promise for the New Testament Church: His only begotten Son, born of a virgin, the King of kings, the Lord of lords, and the Redeemer of man's sins. God knew that we wouldn't follow the Law, and He cares so much about you and me that He gave us a redemptive plan written in the blood of His Son, Jesus. His redemptive plan is neither flawed nor reversible. Look at Galatians:

> Now you're asking yourselves, "So why did God give us the law?" God commanded His heavenly messengers to deliver it into the hand of a mediator for this reason: to help us rein in our sins until the Offspring, about whom the promise was made in the first place, would come (Galatians 3:19, Voice Translation).

Jesus went to the cross for our sins and our physical healing. Some might argue that Jesus was the first promise to the New Testament Church, and when Jesus went to be with the Father, He sent the Holy Spirit, who is the second promise. However, in my opinion, Jesus is the first and the second promise, which is the final and everlasting promise. There will never be another man who will shed his blood for the remission of your sins and mine (Romans 5:17). We don't get another. Aren't you grateful that Jesus was obedient to the redemptive plan made by the Father?

Just think about the obedience Jesus had to show toward the Father and His plan. This was the Father's plan for man's redemption, but Jesus had to agree with the plan for it to be carried out. Even as a small child, I believe Jesus knew that He was born for a special purpose. He certainly knew there was a special calling on His life by the age of twelve. Look at Luke:

> And when he was twelve years old, they went up to Jerusalem after the custom of the feast. And when they had fulfilled the days, as they returned, the child Jesus tarried behind in Jerusalem; and Joseph and his mother knew not of it. But they, supposing him to have been in the company, went a day's journey; and they sought him among their kinsfolk and acquaintance. And when they found him not, they turned back again to Jerusalem, seeking him. And it came to pass, that after three days they found him in the temple, sitting in the midst of the doctors, both hearing them, and asking them questions. And all that heard him were astonished at his understanding and answers. And when they saw him, they were amazed: and his mother said unto him, Son, why hast thou thus dealt with us? behold, thy father and I have sought thee sorrowing. And he said unto them, How is it that ye sought me? wist ye not that I must be about my Father's business? (Luke 2:42-49).

Surely Jesus knew that something special was taking place. Jesus is now practicing fellowship with the Father and the Holy Spirit, which we will also discuss in more detail later.

I would imagine there weren't too many twelve-year-olds doing what Jesus was doing in those days. Just think about the average twelve-year-old child today and what activities they would possibly be involved in. Jesus was obedient to the Father from the exact moment He sensed that He wasn't an ordinary child.

Jesus continued to be obedient to the *Will* of the Father as He grew older. He started His public ministry when He was baptized in the Jordan River by John the Baptist. The Bible says that as He came up out of the water, He saw the heavens open and the Holy Spirit falling on Him like a dove, symbolizing that God was pleased with His obedience (Mark 1:9-11). The dove descending on Him was also a sign that He was The Anointed One as the Messiah by the Holy Spirit. Look at Isaiah:

> The Spirit of the Lord will rest upon him, the Spirit of wisdom and understanding, the Spirit of counsel and power, the Spirit of knowledge and fear of the Lord (Isaiah 11:1-2).

Jesus gave the command to those He appeared not to depart from Jerusalem before they were filled with the Holy Spirit (Luke 24:49, Acts 1:4), but He also gave this command to many of His other followers and, ultimately, gave that same command to the church. The point is, only about 120 were obedient to wait (Acts 1:15). Only those who were obedient were filled, or baptized, with the power of the Holy Spirit.

Our obedience doesn't stop there. After we are filled or baptized with the Holy Spirit, we must be obedient to respond to the voice of the Holy Spirit. We must live in such a way that we never intentionally do anything to cause the Holy Spirit to be grieved or displeased with our actions. But since we are subject to sinning, He will convict us of our wrongdoings. When He does, we must be quick to obey, repent, and make the necessary corrections in our lives. If we are obedient to the commandments of Jesus, you and I can also claim the above Scripture in our life. It is the Holy Spirit that gives wisdom, understanding, counsel, knowledge, and fear of the Lord.

The Promise is Offered to Whosoever

> Then Peter said unto them, Repent, and be baptized every one of you in the name of Jesus Christ for the remission of sins, and ye shall receive the gift of the Holy Ghost. For the promise is unto you, and to your children, and to all that are afar off, even as many as the Lord our God shall call (Acts 2:38-39).

We probably wouldn't be reading the story in Acts about the apostles receiving the Holy Spirit in the Upper Room if they would have gone against Jesus' instructions and not stayed obedient to Him. Peter would not have preached a message where 3,000 souls were saved.

There are many people today who are living way below their promises because they have decided to blame someone else for their shortcomings and failures in life. But the Promise from God is for everyone. It's for your children, their children, and for all the generations that will follow. It's for your neighbors, your friends, and even your enemies. God doesn't leave anyone out. The message of the Promise that Peter preached on that day was not only for those hearing it, but for their family members as well. And He is available today to those that will receive Him and be baptized by Him.

All the other works and miracles that were carried out by the disciples would not have been possible if they had disobeyed the Lord's command. These men were instructed to remain in the Upper Room until the time when the Holy Spirit would appear to be baptized with Him. The Bible does not say how long they waited, but we know that they stayed there long enough to receive the Promise. What if they had grown tired as they did in the garden when Jesus was praying? These men were given an order by the Head of the church, Jesus Christ, to stay in that one place as long as it took until the Father fulfilled His Promise.

I believe we as Christians can learn a lot from the disciple's obedience to stay in the Upper Room to receive the Promise of the Holy Spirit. We can learn that it pays to obey God and His commandments. We can learn that the Promise only comes to those that are hungry and thirsty for it. We can learn that after the Promise is received, it makes us a witness for the Lord. Furthermore, we can learn that we develop a boldness to speak that was not there before.

These men were willing to delay their departure until the Promise was granted, which is unlike many of us today; we are unwilling to wait on the promises of God. It is always better to obey than to make excuses. Sometimes, I wonder what if just *one* of the disciples had doubted and talked the others out of waiting? Would we be reading about the coming of the Promise of the Holy Spirit in some other chapter in Acts or another book of the Bible? Just think about it. If these disciples had not waited on the Promise of the Holy Spirit, the church as we know it today would have been delayed, at least until some other day.

You and I don't have to wait for the Promise of the Holy Spirit. The Promise was fulfilled on the day of Pentecost. All we are required to do is receive Him. When God promises His children something, there is a 110% guarantee that He will not go back on it. It is never God that is wrong or makes a mistake. When His promises to us are not fulfilled or never received, it is without question that the fault lies with us, either in our actions or in some negative influences in our lives.

> Let us hold fast the profession of our faith without wavering; (for he is faithful that promised;) (Hebrew 10:23).

We should never say that God went back on one of His promises. Because God mostly works through humans, if what He had promised toward us ever goes unfilled, it's never because of God. It's always because of something we failed to do or not do or because of something someone else failed to do or not do. Man will look straight into our eyes and lie to us, and most of the time, we have no way of knowing that we're being lied to until after what they had promised goes unfulfilled. Never put too much trust in man's words.

God is not a man, that he should lie; neither the son of man, that he should repent: hath he said, and shall he not do it? or hath he spoken, and shall he not make it good? (Numbers 23:19).

Man's promises are subject to fail and become void, but not God's promises. We can be sure that all of God's promises have already been *willed* to every person who is willing to believe in Him. This includes the infilling or baptism of the Holy Spirit.

The Bible speaks of the New Testament Church as having a better covenant or promise. In Hebrew 8:5-7 it states,

> Who serve unto the example and shadow of heavenly things, as Moses was admonished of God when he was about to make the tabernacle: for, See, saith he, that thou make all things according to the pattern shewed to thee in the mount. But now hath he obtained a more excellent ministry, by how much also he is the mediator of a better covenant, which was established upon better promises. For if that first covenant had been faultless, then should no place have been sought for the second.

The Names of God translation says it like this:

> Yeshua has been given a priestly work that is superior to the Levitical priests' work. He also brings a better promise from God that is based on better guarantees. If nothing had been wrong with the first promise, no one would look for another one (Hebrew 8:6-7, NOG).

There is one word in these verses I want to highlight. That word is "better." Jesus coming to Earth was a *better* covenant and a *better* promise for mankind. What was before was not good enough nor satisfactory for the Father, so He sent us His best, His son, Jesus Christ. But now that Jesus has returned to the Father, the Holy Spirit has come in His place, which God thought was the best substitute for His Son, Jesus. You could say that the Holy Spirit was sent as a surrogate for Jesus Himself. Without the Holy Spirit in this role, we as Christians would be like a fish out of water. The Holy Spirit gives us direction in life.

God, the Creator of the Earth, looked at man and decided that the Old Testament promise, or covenant, was not good enough for you and me. So, He sent His beloved only Son, Jesus, to die on the cross for you and me so that we have a better promise. That promise is Jesus Christ. But because Jesus was obedient to the *Will* of God and could no longer stay on this Earth as a man, He sent us a Helper in His absence—the Holy Spirit —which was the better promise to the church in the absence of Jesus.

There is one last thing that I want to bring to your attention regarding what happens after we are baptized with the Holy Spirit. We receive a boldness to speak for God. Peter, who we have known up to this point, is a person who was not much for speaking out when it came to the things of God. He is remembered more as the disciple who would always put his foot in his mouth, so to speak. But then, after he received the Promise of the Holy Spirit, we see Peter standing up in front of a crowd of at least 3,000 to tell them to repent. We know there were at least 3,000 because that's how many got saved after his sermon, but we don't know that 3,000 represents every person that was there. I'd say that's a new boldness to speak for God.

I am a witness that the Holy Spirit gives you boldness. After I was baptized with Him, He empowered me and gave me a boldness to speak for Christ that I didn't have before. He will do the same for you.

The Promise is for Fellowship and Relationship

Relationships and fellowship are like hands and gloves; they go together. Even though the Holy Spirit lives inside us, if we refuse to build a relationship with Him, we're like the fish that tried to live out of water. We're just flopping through life with no life support. The Holy Spirit is the life support for all believers. The Holy Spirit is there to do the things that we can't do and know the things that we don't know. Let's look at John again:

> I will ask the Father to give[b] you another Helper, to be with you always (John 14:16, International Standard Version).

> Howbeit when he, the Spirit of truth, is come, he will guide you into all truth: for he shall not speak of himself; but whatsoever he shall hear, that shall he speak: and he will shew you things to come (John 16:13).

This is the relationship that every person should want to have with the Holy Spirit. Imagine having a person to help you, guide you, and not just say what they feel or think. The Holy Spirit knows the answer to all of our problems and is waiting to help us. Even the best of friends will sometimes say things that they know they shouldn't, just because they feel that they have a right to do so. Sometimes, people close to us will tell us what we want to hear just to make us feel good, but not the Holy Spirit! He will speak the truth when we don't even know what the truth is.

Relationships are important, but without fellowship, there can't be a relationship. Let me give you an example. Before I married my wife, Brenda, we had to fellowship with each other. Dating is how we fellowshipped; we explored similar interests, did activities together, and had shared feelings and experiences. After some time dating or fellowshipping, we began to develop a relationship with each other. Both of us were in the military, born and raised in the South, and so we decided we shared a common interest in each other. I was interested in her, and she was interested in me. That common interest, along with other factors, led to a committed relationship with each other. As I write this book, that relationship is now 33 years strong and still going. You would have to admit that it would be almost impossible to have a relationship with someone without first having real fellowship with them.

Furthermore, if a married couple lives in the same house with each other and never communicates with each other, there probably won't be a whole lot of fellowship in their relationship. That's not how God intended for a husband and wife to live together. No fellowship, no relationship. It's as simple as that. Paul gave us a good example of how fellowship and relationships work. Look at 2 Corinthians:

> Be ye not unequally yoked together with unbelievers: for what fellowship hath righteousness

unrighteousness? and what communion hath t with darkness? (2 Corinthians 6:14).

ention to the phrase, "for what fellowship." There cannot be fellowship between a believer and an unbeliever because they don't share the same interest. There must be a common sharing of things, and in this case, a common sharing of beliefs, before there can be a relationship between two people.

It works the same way with the Holy Spirit. When we decide to have a fellowship with that Person, the Holy Spirit who lives inside us, an inseparable relationship develops between us. Fellowship with the Holy Spirit produces a power that helps us in our daily life activities. When we need help, all we must do is ask Him for it. When we need direction, He is ready to point us in the right way. When we are confused and looking for answers, He is there to lead us into all truth.

That's why the Holy Spirit desires to have a relationship with you and me. When we get out of fellowship with the Holy Spirit, we tend to limit His involvement in our lives. That's why it's imperative to talk with Him and acknowledge Him in all that we do. It's okay to have one-on-one conversations with the Holy Spirit. I do this daily, mostly by speaking in other tongues. When I use my heavenly prayer language, I speak directly to the Father (1 Corinthians 14:2). Also, the Scripture says that praying in tongues teaches, develops, and acts as a tutor for me (1 Corinthians 14:4a). Things that we don't know but have the desire to know or need to know can be revealed by praying in tongues. Praying in the Holy Spirit reveals the things that are hidden or the things we need clarity with.

In my earlier years as a new Christian, I spent time without fellowship with the Holy Spirit. I knew very little about the Holy Spirit and couldn't fully understand how He could be living inside me and why He wanted to. You must understand that I wasn't a very good person to be around back in those days. There were people that didn't want to be associated with me. And to think that the person of the Holy Spirit desired to live inside me was more than I could wrap my mind around. But I later learned that not only does He desire to live inside me, but He also desires to put up with all my flaws, mistakes, shortcomings, mishaps, sins, etc. He did say that He wouldn't leave nor forsake me (John 14:16, 2 Corinthians 4:9). Whatever I get myself into, the Holy Spirit is present to help me get out of it. What a relationship! But it only happened because I learned to fellowship with Him.

You could say, "Jesus died to have this type of relationship with those who would receive and believe Him." Well, He did die to have a relationship with you and me, but the Holy Spirit desires His own unique relationship with us as well. Look at John again:

> Howbeit when he, the Spirit of truth, is come, he will guide you into all truth: for he shall not speak of himself; but whatsoever he shall hear, that shall he speak: and he will shew you things to come (John 16:13).

In the New Testament Church, the main function of the Holy Spirit is to shed light or illuminate the teachings of Jesus. Not having the Holy Spirit active in our lives is like looking through binoculars without any focus. We would be left to guide ourselves alone through a troubled and confused world where everything appears to be a blur. So while Jesus came to bring us salvation and relationship, the Holy Spirit came for a separate yet equally important purpose: direction and guidance.

Fellowship can be both positive and negative. Positive fellowship means believers having fellowship with the Trinity—Father, Son, and Holy Spirit (John 17:21-23, 1 John 1:3) and with other believers (as we saw in Acts 2:42). When believers have fellowship with Christ, they should have fellowship with one another as well. Fellowship in a negative sense would be believers sharing an unbeliever's lifestyle, which we know ought not to be the case, as mentioned above in 2 Corinthians 6.

One last thing about fellowship with the Holy Spirit. Even though the Holy Spirit knows what we need and knows everything about us, He still desires to have that intimate relationship with us. People sometimes look at themselves and think they have everything they need, that they don't need the help of anyone else. Other people might look at them as well and think that they have all the answers and that they've got their life together. Because of their own misconceptions about themselves and because of the perceptions they think others have about them, they refuse to ask for help when they desperately need it. And the sad part is, no one will offer help to them either. Even their best friend might not think or realize the need to offer any assistance. However, the Holy Spirit is just the opposite. He always knows when we have need of Him and is always ready to lend a helping hand to us. This is the intimate relationship I'm speaking about. He is always extending His hand, even when we think we don't need help. Jesus has something to say about knowing what we have need of. Take a look at Matthew:

> Behold the fowls of the air: for they sow not, neither do they reap, nor gather into barns; yet your heavenly Father feedeth them. Are ye not much better than they? Which of you by taking thought can add one cubit unto his stature? And why take ye thought for raiment? Consider the lilies of the field, how they grow; they toil not, neither do they spin: And yet I say unto you, That even Solomon in all his glory was not arrayed like one of these. Wherefore, if God so clothe the grass of the field, which to day is, and to morrow is cast into the oven, shall he not much more clothe you, O ye of little faith? Therefore take no thought, saying, What shall we eat? or, What shall we drink? or, Wherewithal shall we be clothed? (For after all these things do the Gentiles seek:) for your heavenly Father knoweth that ye have need of all these things (Matthew 6:26-32).

As believers, we should never be ashamed to ask the Holy Spirit for help. Remember, that is just one of the responsibilities. John 14:26, the International Standard Version, describes Him as a Helper. So, when you and I aren't even aware that we need something, the Holy Spirit knows. And even if we *are* aware that we need something, He knew about it long before we had to ask.

The Promise is Accompanied by a Teacher

We've already looked at John 14:26, but let's examine it again:

> But the Comforter, which is the Holy Ghost, whom the Father will send in my name, he shall teach you all things, and bring all things to your remembrance, whatsoever I have said unto you.

First, let's discuss the teacher. Remember, the Holy Spirit, Jesus, and the Father are a three-in-one Person. When Jesus was on Earth, part of His ministry was to teach (Matthew 4:23). The Father teaches us through His Word. These three are still teaching us, even today. Imagine always having a teacher by your side. Someone you can talk to, ask questions, and get instructions or advice from. This type of education is priceless. It's more valuable than any Bible school, college, or seminary. But notice what John 14:26 says, "he shall teach you all things."

You might say, "I don't want to know all things." Well, neither should anyone. But the "all things" He's speaking of here are teaching you all the things of the Spirit and bringing to your remembrance all the words that Jesus spoke while He was on Earth. Imagine having someone with you all the time whose sole purpose is to teach you all things about Jesus and the Holy Spirit.

Teachers are masters in their field of study. Jesus is not just a teacher, but He's also the one and only Master of all things concerning the Holy Spirit in our lives. Have you ever had something in your life that you didn't understand or just needed more information on? The Holy Spirit is promised to provide us wisdom, revelation, knowledge, and insight on the things you and I wouldn't otherwise know or understand. God intended for all of us who believe to receive the Promise of the Holy Spirit.

The Holy Spirit is there not only to teach you all things but also to help you recall important, necessary details. Have you ever forgotten something, lost something, or just forgotten where you placed something? I know I have. Well, you and I have a supernatural force that lives inside us and knows everything from beginning to end. The Holy Spirit, metaphorically speaking, will bring everything to our remembrance (John 14:26). He is the best reminder that anyone could hope for.

Life itself can be a test at times. We sometimes struggle with making daily decisions. Should I do this or do that? Should I go there or not? Every day, life decisions can be a challenge. Considering all the voices in the world today, if we aren't in fellowship with and have a relationship with the Holy Spirit, there's a good chance we will make the wrong choice. I have good news, though. When we are faced with a series of tests, we always have a Test-Taker with us, and He has never failed one. He has all the right answers, He goes wherever we go, and He'll do whatever we ask. He's the master Teacher, and there is no test that you and I will face during this life that He hasn't already passed. Imagine if you were in high school or college, and your teacher or professor wasn't as smart as you. It would be somewhat counter-productive to continue to listen to them and follow their teaching. Why? Any student that's smarter or knows more about the subject matter has no need for a teacher or professor. But, when the teacher or professor has the knowledge and wisdom that the student needs to pass the course or get to the next level, then they'll diligently listen and obey.

So, as a student of the Holy Spirit, believers are to remain mindful and be all ears. We shouldn't be inattentive to the teaching of the Holy Spirit. For us to get all the information we need from the master Teacher, we must be willing to show up to class and submit ourselves to His teaching. Showing up to the Holy Spirit classroom can take on many forms. Some examples are reading the Bible, meditating on the Word, praying in the Holy Spirit, and church attendance. You could say that someone who participates in these activities is a disciplined student. For you and me to get all we need from the Holy Spirit, we must be disciplined students. Look at Luke:

> Students are not greater than their teachers. But the student who is fully trained will become like the teacher (Luke 6:40, New Living Translation).

Now, you and I know that we will never be a fraction of who Jesus was, but we can be imitators of Him by learning from and living by what He taught us. The Holy Spirit is the master Teacher, and we're the students in need of His knowledge, wisdom, understanding, etc. He desires that we share like-mindedness. Look at 1 Corinthians:

> But God hath revealed them unto us by his Spirit: for the Spirit searcheth all things, yea, the deep things of God. For what man knoweth the things of a man, save the spirit of man which is in him? even so the things of God knoweth no man, but the Spirit of God. Now we have received, not the spirit of the world, but the spirit which is of God; that we might know the things that are freely given to us of God. Which

> things also we speak, not in the words which man's wisdom teacheth, but which the Holy Ghost teacheth; comparing spiritual things with spiritual. But the natural man receiveth not the things of the Spirit of God: for they are foolishness unto him: neither can he know them, because they are spiritually discerned. But he that is spiritual judgeth all things, yet he himself is judged of no man. For who hath known the mind of the Lord, that he may instruct him? But we have the mind of Christ (1 Corinthians 2:10-16).

Things of the Spirit cannot be taught by the words of man. Man speaks spiritual things only through the Holy Spirit that lives inside of him. A person that is baptized with the Holy Spirit can discern the things of God and judge the words that man speaks. Many believers don't have the Holy Spirit living inside them and operating in this way. They cannot discern the spirit of others because they don't have the Holy Spirit to tell them otherwise.

Let us look at another example of the Holy Spirit as a teacher. We see in Acts 1:5 that the baptism of the Holy Spirit is the flow of the Spirit's power for the work of missions and evangelism. The Holy Spirit teaches Christians how to witness, proclaim His gospel, and lead others to Christ. The Bible also says that the Holy Spirit compels one to confess Jesus as Lord (1 Corinthians 12:3). We see from this verse that the Holy Spirit is the person who causes us to acknowledge who Jesus is so that we can receive salvation. This is one of the greatest teaching moments in a person's life. Why? Because Romans 10:10 says,

> For with the heart man believeth unto righteousness; and with the mouth confession is made unto salvation.

Scriptures also tell us that the Holy Spirit teaches us the deep things of God (1 Corinthians 2:10-12) and the secrets of Christ (Ephesians 3:3-5). In other words, the Holy Spirit teaches us the hearts of God and Christ. He teaches us things about God and Christ that we could never know otherwise. God and Jesus desire that we know all there is to know about them. When we don't know what to say, the Holy Spirit teaches us what to say in the moment we need to speak (Luke 12:12). The Holy Spirit releases a power that's available to us to be witnesses to Him and for Him.

The Promise Offers Other Spiritual Gifts

The Promise of the Holy Spirit is a gift given to the church by Jesus from the Father. But along with the Promise of the Holy Spirit, other spiritual gifts are available to those that receive the gift of the Holy Spirit. These gifts are given to the church to secure its strength and unity. These spiritual gifts and the manifestations of the gifts are recorded in 1 Corinthians 12:1-11:

> Now concerning spiritual gifts, brethren, I would not have you ignorant. Ye know that ye were Gentiles, carried away unto these dumb idols, even as ye were led. Wherefore I give you to understand, that no man speaking by the Spirit of God calleth Jesus accursed: and that no man can say that Jesus is the Lord but by the Holy Ghost. Now there are diversities of gifts, but the same Spirit. And there are differences of

administrations, but the same Lord. And there are diversities of operations, but it is the same God which worketh all in all. But the manifestation of the Spirit is given to every man to profit withal. For to one is given by the Spirit the word of wisdom; to another the word of knowledge by the same Spirit; To another faith by the same Spirit; to another the gifts of healing by the same Spirit; To another the working of miracles; to another prophecy; to another discerning of spirits; to another divers kinds of tongues; to another the interpretation of tongues: But all these worketh that one and the selfsame Spirit, dividing to every man severally as he will.

As you can see from the verses above, there are nine gifts of the Spirit that are available to every person after they're baptized with the Holy Spirit. The Holy Spirit that the disciples were told to wait for in the Upper Room is the same Spirit from whom these nine gifts originate. Any of these nine gifts can be bestowed upon you, but they are granted by the Holy Spirit, as the Spirit wills, which Jesus promised the disciples on the Day of Pentecost. Notice what verse seven from the passage above states:

> But all these worketh that one and the selfsame Spirit, dividing to every man severally as he will (1 Corinthians 12:7).

These gifts of the Spirit cannot be bought or received in any other way except by the baptism of the Holy Spirit. Unfortunately, some have thought that these gifts could be bought. After Peter had preached the message where 3,000 souls were saved, there were some that offered to buy the gifts of the Spirit. The Book of Acts details the events of this story:

> Saying, Give me also this power, that on whomsoever I lay hands, he may receive the Holy Ghost. But Peter said unto him, Thy money perish with thee, because thou hast thought that the gift of God may be purchased with money. Thou hast neither part nor lot in this matter: for thy heart is not right in the sight of God (Acts 8:19-21).

Another translation says it like this:

> Simon noticed that the Spirit was given only when the apostles placed their hands on the people. So, he brought money and said to Peter and John, "Let me have this power too! Then anyone I place my hands on will also be given the Holy Spirit. Peter said to him, "You and your money will both end up in hell if you think you can buy God's gift! You don't have any part in this, and God sees that your heart isn't right (Acts 8: 18-21, CVE).

Nothing that God has promised His children can be bought with any amount of money or good works. Never think that you or I can receive the promised gifts of the Spirit other than by being baptized with the Holy Spirit and receiving the gifts from Him as a result. The Promise of the Holy Spirit is sent for whosoever will believe and receive Jesus Christ as their Lord and Savior. After you're born again, you're now a candidate for being filled with the Holy Spirit and operating in all, one, or some combination of the nine gifts mentioned in 1 Corinthians 12.

Chapter 2
The Presence and Power of the Holy Spirit

The first recorded story of the presence of the Holy Spirit since the Promise was given is found in the Book of Acts. This is where we'll explore the Presence and Power of the Holy Spirit. This is about the rushing, mighty wind that filled the room. Let's examine Acts 2 again:

> And when the day of Pentecost was fully come, they were all with one accord in one place. And suddenly there came a sound from heaven as of a rushing mighty wind, and it filled all the house where they were sitting. And there appeared unto them cloven tongues like as of fire, and it sat upon each of them. And they were all filled with the Holy Ghost, and began to speak with other tongues, as the Spirit gave them utterance (Acts 2:1-4).

In the above verse, the sound of a rushing, mighty wind is the presence of the Holy Spirit. This is when He filled the house and when they were all filled too. Like we said before, not only was the house filled, but they were also filled with the Holy Spirit. This caused them to speak in other tongues. Then, there were cloven tongues like fire that appeared unto them. This is the first of many appearances of the Holy Spirit since the Promise of Him was announced by Jesus prior to His ascension to the Father. We'll continue to discuss the book of Acts a little later, but first I want to share a story with you about the Presence and Power of the Holy Spirit.

Obedience is Necessary for the Power

We have already discussed how obedience to God is necessary to receive the Promise. Likewise, obedience is also necessary to create the Power of the Holy Spirit. Without our obedience to His commands and nudging, we would be like fish trying to live outside of water. There is a story in the Bible about men fishing in the Lake of Gennesaret. Look at Luke:

> And it came to pass, that, as the people pressed upon him to hear the word of God, he stood by the lake of Gennesaret, And saw two ships standing by the lake: but the fishermen were gone out of them, and were washing their nets. And he entered into one of the ships, which was Simon's, and prayed him that he would thrust out a little from the land. And he sat down, and taught the people out of the ship. Now when he had left speaking, he said unto Simon, Launch out into the deep, and let down your nets for a draught. And Simon answering said unto him, Master, we have toiled all the night, and have taken nothing: nevertheless at thy word I will let down the net. And when they had this done, they inclosed a great multitude of fishes: and their net brake (Luke 5:1-6).

This is a story about how a fisherman named Simon who was obedient to the words of Jesus and the result of his obedience. Apparently, these two ships had been out together all night fishing but had no success in catching any fish. No doubt these men were tired and wanted to anchor their boats to get some rest. Right in the midst of them calling it a night, Jesus steps on Simon's boat and begins to give him commands. What happened next depended on Simon's response.

First, Jesus commanded Simon to propel the boat a little further out into the water. Jesus wanted to get offshore a little further so His teachings could be more effective. This was Simon's first opportunity to obey or disobey the words of Jesus. Keep in mind now that at this point, Jesus had already been baptized with the Holy Spirit (Matthew 3:16), so the commands He's giving Simon are produced by the Power of the Holy Spirit. Simon obeys the first command. As soon Jesus had finished teaching the people, He gave Simon a second command: to go even further out into the waters and drop his nets.

Simon expresses his frustrations with the commands of Jesus and lets Him know how he feels about them. You must understand that Simon and the other men were experienced fishermen and knew how to catch fish. This is how these men made a living. If we were them, we probably would've thought, "Man, I am tired and ready to go to sleep. What does He know about fishing?" Well, they're about to find out.

Even though Simon was exhausted from being on the lake all night long without catching any fish, he did as Jesus commanded: he launched out into the deep and let down his nets. After Simon obeyed Jesus, he experienced the Power of the Holy Spirit through the words of Jesus. Simon could have easily missed out on his blessing of a boatload of fish. Not only was Simon blessed with fish, but also all the men that had been out on the lake with him that night. They hadn't had success either, but they were blessed too.

This is the Power of the Holy Spirit in manifestation. When we obey the leadership of the Holy Spirit, a power comes upon us to do things that are uncommon. Notice, though, that the Power is not just for you and me but also for those around us. Because of Simon's obedience, he and his fishermen friends had enough fish to feed their families as well as sell to the local fish market so that others could buy them and feed their families. All of this happened because of one man's obedience to the words produced by the Power of the Holy Spirit. Remember that the Holy Spirit left Saul because of his disobedience (1 Samuel 16:14).

Story #1: The Lost Purse

One Saturday morning in the summer of 1997, I got a phone call from my wife, Brenda, around 10 a.m. She said that she couldn't find her purse after running some errands and returning home. At the time, I was still serving in the military and had taken on a part-time job at a local automotive parts store. I had gone to work early that morning. So when she told me what happened, I immediately thought, "Now, why would I know where her purse was?" Of course, I didn't say that to her, but I remember telling her not to worry and that we would find it, and that I was on my way home.

When I arrived home, I remember asking her where and when she remembered last seeing it. She explained where she was when she last had it in her possession and where she had been since. I immediately jumped into my truck and drove the route she had taken that morning. The whole time I was praying in another tongue. There was one location on the road where I felt compelled to stop and look, so I got out and started walking around and looking.

After a few minutes of walking and looking along the grassy roadside, I heard these words in my spirit: "Go back home and pray with your wife." At first, I started to ignore what I had heard and justify to God why that was not a good idea. Then I heard those same words again, "Go back home and pray with your wife." This time, it was different. It sounded like there was more authority in the words. This time, I was sure that it was not me just hearing things but something much bigger. I needed to do exactly what I had heard.

Those words, "Go back home and pray with your wife," were the Presence of the Holy Spirit coming forth to assist me in finding my wife's purse. But notice, I almost let His help slip away by disobeying what I heard the first time. I was ignoring the voice of the Holy Spirit, which can effectively extinguish it. The Bible calls it quenching the Spirit (1 Thessalonians 5:19). So, what does He do next? He appears to me again with the same words, "Go back home and pray with your wife."

Just as the Holy Spirit led Jesus into the wilderness (Luke 4:4), the Holy Spirit living inside me was so concerned about my worries that He was willing to present Himself to me as many times as it took to get my attention. Thank God it only took two attempts before I obeyed. I wonder how many times the Holy Spirit has tried to get our attention, and we just ignore or miss His directing? I know I've missed His leadership and direction in my life as a believer. I'm thankful He was there on the side of the road with me that day. He will do the same for you. After all, He is our Helper.

The second time I didn't hesitate to get in my truck and drive back home. I was still praying in the spirit. When I got home, the first thing Brenda asked me was, "Did you find it?" I replied, "No." She was probably thinking, "Well, why are you back here then?" I told her that we were supposed to pray and ask the Holy Spirit where her purse was. I prayed with her like I was instructed to, and she agreed to do the same. I still remember the verses in Mark that I prayed:

> For verily I say unto you, That whosoever shall say unto this mountain, Be thou removed, and be thou cast into the sea; and shall not doubt in his heart, but shall believe that those things which he saith shall come to pass; he shall have whatsoever he saith. Therefore I say unto you, What things soever ye desire, when ye pray, believe that ye receive them, and ye shall have them (Mark 11:23-24).

I also asked the Holy Spirit to show us where Brenda had left her purse and for it to be returned with nothing missing. You might be reading this and saying, "You asked the Holy Spirit?" Yes, I asked Him point blank. You read it right. John explains that we can and should do that:

> Verily, verily, I say unto you, He that believeth on me, the works that I do shall he do also; and greater works than these shall he do; because I go unto my Father. And whatsoever ye shall ask in my name,

that will I do, that the Father may be glorified in the Son. If ye shall ask anything in my name, I will do it. If ye love me, keep my commandments (John 12-15).

He said if I ask anything in His name, he would do it, but there are two qualifiers. They are: loving Him and keeping His commandments. If we love Him and follow His teachings, then we can ask the Holy Spirit anything, as long as it doesn't go against His will, which is God's Word.

I could feel and sense the presence of the Holy Spirit the whole time up to this point. After we had finished praying, I went back to work and dropped Brenda off at her hair appointment. She had transportation, but because her driver's license was in her purse, we didn't want her to be driving. When she got out of the truck, I said to her, "When we get back home, there will be a message on the phone's answering machine from someone saying that they found your purse." It was the Power of the Holy Spirit that caused me to say those words. It was not my power or might that caused me to say those words, but by the Power of the Holy Spirit. I couldn't have made this up even if I wanted to. There is a story in Zechariah that illustrates this point:

> And the angel that talked with me came again, and waked me, as a man that is wakened out of his sleep. And said unto me, What seest thou? And I said, I have looked, and behold a candlestick all of gold, with a bowl upon the top of it, and his seven lamps thereon, and seven pipes to the seven lamps, which are upon the top thereof: And two olive trees by it, one upon the right side of the bowl, and the other upon the left side thereof. So I answered and spoke

to the angel that talked with me, saying, What are these, my lord? Then the angel that talked with me answered and said unto me, Knowest thou not what these be? And I said, No, my lord. Then he answered and spake unto me, saying, This is the word of the Lord unto Zerubbabel, saying, Not by might, nor by power, but by my spirit, saith the Lord of hosts (Zechariah 4:1-6).

Zechariah was an Old Testament prophet and, at one point, the king of Israel (2 Kings 14:29). During Zechariah's reign as king of Israel, Zerubbabel was governor of Judah. After returning from the Captivity of Babylon, Zerubbabel and the people of Judah were procrastinating on rebuilding the Temple. One thing came up after another, which delayed the rebuilding of the Temple. We know how it is in our own lives. As the saying goes, "Life happens." We don't know whether they were being disobedient or just plain lazy. I can imagine hearing Zerubbabel and the people complaining and saying things like, "We'll never get this Temple rebuilt," or, "We just don't have the time or the resources to rebuild this Temple." You know how we do sometimes when it seems like life is dealing us more than we can handle!

Whatever the reasons were, Zerubbabel needed a little encouragement to get them going, and they got that through the prophet Zechariah. Remember, we already established that in the Old Testament, the Holy Spirit came upon or entered the prophets of God when God wanted to use them to speak to His people. After God was done speaking, the Holy Spirit departed them.

The Holy Spirit is not someone to be ignored. It's imperative for a believer who has been baptized with the Holy Spirit not to neglect the leadership of the Holy Spirit. If we, as believers filled with the Holy Spirit, fail to acknowledge the voice of the Holy Spirit, He will cease to speak to us at some point. The Holy Spirit departed from Saul because of his disobedience (1 Samuel 16:14). Because the Holy Spirit is the demonstrated Power of the Trinity, the Bible tells us not to grieve Him (Ephesians 4:30). The Holy Spirit loves a peaceful and gentle relationship. That's why He is referred to as a dove in the Scripture, which we already covered. Likewise, you and I will no longer have fellowship or a relationship with the Holy Spirit if we are disobedient and reject His involvement in our lives.

As I mentioned earlier, we are not to grieve the Holy Spirit. We are also told not to quench the Holy Spirit (1 Thessalonians 5:19). I like what this translation says:

> Don't try to stop what the Holy Spirit is doing (1 Thessalonians 5:19, New International Reader's Version).

The Holy Spirit was sent by the Father for the purpose of helping believers through this life, which we find in John 16:13. Ever since I was filled with the Holy Spirit, with the evidence of speaking in other tongues, He has been the equipping force I needed. I want the Holy Spirit to do the work in my life that He was sent to do. I don't want to do anything to make Him feel unwelcome at any point in time. We have already seen that the Holy Spirit came upon Zechariah by way of an angel from God and instructed him to tell Zerubbabel that the Lord's Temple shall be built. The Holy Spirit was saying that the Temple would be built by the authority and the power of the Spirit of God. It would not be built by secular means or by using man's policies. No education, no degree, no other means, but only by His Spirit.

Ephesians 4:30 also tells us that the Holy Spirit seals us until the day of redemption. Believers are told not to do anything to hurt or make the Holy Spirit sad because He's there to keep us from evil, rescue us when we fall into danger, and preserve us until the day of Jesus' return for His church.

There are times in all of our lives when we are faced with circumstances that seem to be out of our control, and we can't see any way out. I'm here to tell you that we have a supernatural power living inside of us that is there to help and assist. All we must do is dispatch Him to the rescue.

Now, back to the lost purse story. You must understand that I was still on active duty, and Brenda had a military-dependent ID card in her purse. Back then, anyone losing their military ID card was not taken lightly by the military. It was mainly a security issue. I'm sure you can understand why. But she also had other important information in it, like her driver's license, credit card, and other important papers containing her personal information. Just the military ID card alone was enough to get me a little agitated and in strife with Brenda. But I remembered what the two verses say following Mark 11: 23-24:

> And when ye stand praying, forgive, if ye have ought against any: that your Father also which is in heaven may forgive you your trespasses. But if ye do not forgive, neither will your Father which is in heaven forgive your trespasses (Mark 11:25-26).

I forgave Brenda for the predicament that she had put me in. I say "me" because I would be the one held accountable for the lost ID card. As bad as this incident appeared to be, I never felt troubled or concerned about it. Why? Well, I was never worried because I had heard from my Helper, the Holy Spirit. He instructed me on what to do, and I entrusted Him completely, doing exactly as I was told. I knew that it was the Holy Spirit living inside me that helped me forgive Brenda at that very moment. Look at what John has to say about forgiveness through the Holy Spirit:

> Now having received the Holy Spirit, and being led and directed by Him, if you forgive the sins of anyone, they are forgiven; if you retain the sins of anyone, they are retained (John 20:23, Amplified Bible, Classic Edition).

Now, remember that as Brenda and I departed that morning and I dropped her off at her appointment, I said some very specific words to her. I had said, "When we get back home, there will be a message on the phone's answering machine from someone saying that they found your purse." After that, I acted like nothing had happened and went back to my job.

Once my shift ended, I picked Brenda up, and we drove home. We may have talked about her purse, but it wasn't a real serious conversation. We arrived home shortly after. When we opened the door and walked into the house, the phone's answering machine was beeping. Hallelujah! I can hardly contain myself as I write this. We heard the beeping from the answering machine, and I looked at Brenda and said, "Check the message." She hit the button, and there was a message on the machine. Not two! Just one. Can you guess what the message said? It went something like this: "Hello, (she gave her name). My husband and I found a purse that we believe belongs to you. Please call us."

It took us a moment to get control of our emotions. We were thanking God and rejoicing in the fact that someone had found Brenda's purse. After we regained our composure, Brenda called the phone number left by the lady on the answering machine. The lady told Brenda that she and her husband lived in Crossville, Tennessee but were in Knoxville, Tennessee, for yard sales hopping and had found her purse lying in the middle of the road at an intersection.

We got her address, got in our vehicle, and drove 45 minutes to Crossville. When we arrived at their house, we all greeted one another. The Holy Spirit had used wonderful people to help us. After a little while of talking, we learned that Brenda's purse was found less than 50 yards from our driveway. The way this situation turned out was because of the power of the Holy Spirit working on our behalf. All I did was get Him involved. He wants to be involved with your life struggles, too. Let's revisit a verse in John:

> But the Comforter, which is the Holy Ghost, whom the Father will send in my name, he shall teach you all things, and bring all things to your remembrance, whatsoever I have said unto you (John 14:26).

Jesus said He would not leave me disheartened, depressed, dreary, or without answers but would come to me. Let's look at another example of the Presence of the Holy Spirit. If you read my book, "A God-Balanced Life," you'll recall the story I shared with you when Brenda and I were stranded on the side of the road because our car stopped running. This story about the lost purse is similar. In the same way, the Holy Spirit worked through me to rescue us that early morning by telling me to flag down a car, which turned out to be a relative of mine on my mother's side. He did the same thing to assist in the recovery of Brenda's purse. I think you would enjoy the book if you haven't read it before.

There have been many days in my walk with God that I have been in situations where I was unable to produce results in my own strength or power and needed help. The Bible talks about the Holy Spirit helping in our infirmities (Romans 8:26). In the stories I just shared with you about the lost purse and about us being stranded on the side of the road, there is clear evidence of the Holy Spirit helping in my infirmities. According to Vine's Complete Expository Dictionary, the word "infirmity" means want of strength; weakness, indicating an inability to produce results. Have you ever been in a spot where you needed extra strength because you couldn't do something in your own power?

Imagine you were struggling to lift a very heavy object, and you needed help. One of your best friends comes to you and says, "Friend, I see you need some help. Would you like me to help you?" You reply, "Sure, thank you." After all, who would turn down some much-needed help? So, you'd get on one side of the object, and your friend would get on the other side. You'd both grab hold of the object and lift it at the same time. What was too heavy for you alone is now easy to lift because you have help.

Likewise, this is what the Holy Spirit does for us. When we're in need of help and we invite Him to help, He comes along beside us and shares our pains, struggles, sorrows, hurts, confusions, shortcomings, and anything else we need help with. Let's look at a verse in Romans a little closer:

> Likewise, the Spirit also helpeth our infirmities: for we know not what we should pray for as we ought: but the Spirit itself maketh intercession for us with groanings which cannot be uttered (Romans 8:26).

Notice that the Holy Spirit doesn't relieve us of our responsibility and leaves all the work for Himself. Instead, He says, "I can help you, but you must do your part. Use your faith, believe, pray in other tongues, and I'll come alongside you and lift with you. Both of us working together will solve your problem." The phrase "helpeth our infirmities" means exactly what it says. He helps us, but He also gets us involved and keeps us involved. Therefore, it's important for believers to be baptized with the Holy Spirit with the evidence of speaking in other tongues. If we speak in other tongues, we can also pray in other tongues.

The Holy Spirit gives believers of Christ the wisdom to help them understand things of God. The Holy Spirit searches the heart of God. When we're unable to get results on our own, the Holy Spirit can. When we have done all that we know to do, such as pray and fast, and there are still no results, it's time to dispatch the Holy Spirit to assist you in your problem. We've already looked at 1 Corinthians 2, but the following verses warrant another look:

> But God hath revealed them unto us by his Spirit: for the Spirit searcheth all things, yea, the deep things of God. For what man knoweth the things of a man, save the spirit of man which is in him? even so the things of God knoweth no man, but the Spirit of God (1 Corinthians 2:10-11).

The only way a believer in Christ can fully know God is by having the Holy Spirit living inside them. Indeed, we know

Him from His Word, but I'm speaking of a level that goes much deeper than just the new birth. By the works of the Holy Spirit, God helps believers be aware of things that they wouldn't know by natural means. He reveals these things to us by the Spirit (1 Cor. 2:10), which is the Holy Spirit. It is the Holy Spirit, through the Word of God, that believers come to acknowledge, understand, and apply the heart of God to our situation.

There is one more thing I want to point out about the Holy Spirit in my lost purse story, which is: He is a guide. Look at John:

> Howbeit when he, the Spirit of truth, is come, he will guide you into all truth: for he shall not speak of himself; but whatsoever he shall hear, that shall he speak: and he will shew you things to come (John 16:13).

When I was walking alongside that road, praying in other tongues, I heard the words, "Go back home and pray with your wife." That was the Holy Spirit guiding me to the truth about where Brenda's purse was and how to get it back. Plus, telling Brenda there would be a message on the answering machine was His way of showing me what the future outcome would be.

We have a Helper working with us while we wait for our delivery, whatever that may be at different times in our lives. When we don't know what to pray in English, the Holy Spirit helps us by praying for us and interceding for us with unspoken groanings. I'm glad that the Holy Spirit prays for me when I don't know what to pray for. What I mean is, I don't know the Holy Spirit's language of prayer like He does. If we're children of the Kingdom of God, then we're not of this world (John 18:36). Without the Holy Spirit, we would be like outsiders, strolling around in a country without any help. But, because we have the Holy Spirit, we have a Helper who can translate between our spirit and the Spirit of God.

When I think about all the details of what took place that day, I sometimes wonder why the information about the purse wasn't given to Brenda. She was baptized with the Holy Spirit just as I was. Why didn't the Holy Spirit speak to her and reveal to her the details that He revealed to me? I wasn't any more spiritual than she was. Why did He choose to speak to me? I don't have the answer to those questions. The older I get and the more I experience the goodness of God, I find myself recalling and reflecting on the things God has done for me in the past. One of the things I have come to realize is this: if He did it once, He'll do it again and again.

One day I was pondering on the lost purse situation and how it was recovered. As I was rehearsing what had happened that day, I finally got some insight. I think I now have a pretty good idea of why I was chosen to be the mouthpiece for the Holy Spirit. It was simply because I was the one the Holy Spirit chose that day. Let's look at 1 Corinthians again:

> But all these worketh that one and the selfsame Spirit, dividing to every man severally as he will (1 Corinthians 12:11).

The words the Holy Spirit gave me when I was walking alone on that road is what's called a Word of Knowledge. The book of 1 Corinthians, chapter 12, explains to us the spiritual gifts provided for the church by the Holy Spirit. We don't choose the spiritual gift of our liking. It's the Holy Spirit that gives as He sees fit. He spoke to me that day because He chose to, and He knew my whole heart's desire was for Brenda to have peace and comfort. Even though I asked, He already knew what I needed. You and I can trust Him to come to our aid in times of need. By me trusting Him that day, I was able to serve Brenda.

On the other hand, I could have missed what He was saying to me. I'm thankful that my mind was free of the cares of this world and personal issues that could have shut off my spirit from the Holy Spirit. Look at Mark:

> And the cares of this world, and the deceitfulness of riches, and the lusts of other things entering in, choke the word, and it becometh unfruitful (Mark 4:19).

I think many times, we allow the cares of life to distort our vision, and we forget that we have the greater One living inside us. When this happens, we fail to hear what the Holy Spirit is saying, and we, therefore, miss our assignment.

I know that speaking in different tongues idly has turned a lot of people away but look at it as speaking the wisdom of God. When we speak in other tongues, we're speaking God's wisdom into our situation where we were unable to get results. The entire chapter of 1 Corinthians 2 tells us this:

> And I, brethren, when I came to you, came not with excellency of speech or of wisdom, declaring unto you the testimony of God. For I determined not to know anything among you, save Jesus Christ, and him crucified. And I was with you in weakness, and in fear, and in much trembling. And my speech and my preaching was not with enticing words of man's

wisdom, but in demonstration of the Spirit and of power (1 Corinthians 2:1-4).

In these first five verses alone, Paul declares that his speech was not of his own wisdom or another man's wisdom, but it was from the wisdom that the Holy Spirit produced through His Power. Paul's goal was not to impress the people with his lucid speech, but more importantly, he wanted the people to understand the message of Jesus Christ and His crucifixion. So, we can see from the verses above that the Holy Spirit provides the believer with the wisdom of Jesus Christ. Paul was one hundred percent dependent on the Holy Spirit to get his message across to the people and to make it convincing. Let's look further at Corinthians:

> That your faith should not stand in the wisdom of men, but in the power of God. Howbeit we speak wisdom among them that are perfect: yet not the wisdom of this world, nor of the princes of this world, that come to nought: But we speak the wisdom of God in a mystery, even the hidden wisdom, which God ordained before the world unto our glory: Which none of the princes of this world knew: for had they known it, they would not have crucified the Lord of glory (1 Corinthians 2:5-8).

Furthermore, we see from the verses above that he goes on to tell the Corinthian believers that God isn't against the wisdom of men but rather that God is where his wisdom comes from. God's desire for believers to seek His wisdom is provided by the Holy Spirit. I personally know elderly people who have great wisdom for living a successful life that they have experienced firsthand, but if their wisdom goes against the wisdom of God, I must use the latter as my source of wisdom.

My own father, who went home to be with Jesus at the age of 95, gave me great wisdom up until his last days on earth. As much as I loved my father and welcomed his, many times, unsolicited wisdom, it didn't supersede the wisdom of the Holy Spirit. Paul's wisdom was based on the wisdom he received from the Holy Spirit, and believers should do the same.

> But as it is written, Eye hath not seen, nor ear heard, neither have entered into the heart of man, the things which God hath prepared for them that love him. But God hath revealed them unto us by his Spirit: for the Spirit searcheth all things, yea, the deep things of God. For what man knoweth the things of a man, save the spirit of man which is in him? Even so, the things of God knoweth no man, but the Spirit of God (1 Corinthians 2:9-11).

God can make things known to those that believe through His Holy Spirit that they would otherwise never know. Not even the human heart can receive such things. Many believers may think this verse is a reference to when they get to Heaven, but it's actually for the right-now life. This is how God explains who He is through the wisdom of the Holy Spirit. The Bible says,

> For my thoughts are not your thoughts, neither are your ways my ways, saith the Lord. For as the heavens are higher than the earth, so are my ways higher than your ways, and my thoughts than your thoughts (Isaiah 55:8-9).

Since we believers don't think the way that God thinks, and we don't know His ways, we depend on the Holy Spirit to lead and guide us.

> Now we have received, not the spirit of the world, but the spirit which is of God; that we might know the things that are freely given to us of God. Which things also we speak, not in the words which man's wisdom teacheth, but which the Holy Ghost teacheth; comparing spiritual things with spiritual. But the natural man receiveth not the things of the Spirit of God: for they are foolishness unto him: neither can he know them, because they are spiritually discerned. But he that is spiritual judgeth all things, yet he himself is judged of no man. For who hath known the mind of the Lord, that he may instruct him? but we have the mind of Christ (1 Corinthians 2:12-16).

The Holy Spirit's wisdom is always better than wisdom gained from worldly living. Worldly doing and thinking don't lead us to the doorway of God's way of doing and thinking. When believers try to use the world's wisdom to connect with what God desires to do or how He thinks, it's like trying to connect their computers to the internet without an internet service provider. All they get is a blank screen with some words explaining the problem. It would be foolish to expect internet service without an internet connection. A believer's connection with the things of God is having the Holy Spirit present and active in their life. What is provided to believers through the Holy Spirit is given to them freely by God Himself. Once again, all believers have the Spirit of God living inside them, but not all believers have been baptized with the Holy Spirit. I believe this is where the line is drawn between whether a believer can discern the things of God or not. No one knows the mind of God like the Holy Spirit.

Story #2: Jesus Turns Water into Wine

As we mentioned before, Jesus was born of the Holy Ghost (Matthew 1:18), but it was still necessary for Him to be baptized with the Holy Spirit. Jesus, the Head of the church, did not perform any miracles until He was baptized with the Holy Spirit. First, Jesus was water baptized by John the Baptist (Matthew 3:13-17), but then, the Bible says that when He came out of the water, the heavens were opened, and He could see the Spirit of God descending like a dove and a light shining upon him (3:16). This is the Presence and Power of the Holy Spirit. This is when Jesus was baptized with the Holy Spirit of the Father. This is the same Holy Spirit Jesus promised to believers after He went to the Father. Look at the next verse:

> And lo a voice from heaven, saying, This is my beloved Son, in whom I am well pleased (Matthew 3:17).

I'm not suggesting that when a believer is water baptized, he is baptized with the Holy Spirit at the same time. Neither am I saying that it couldn't happen at water baptism. However, that was the case for Jesus. Jesus heard the Father's voice. I wonder what the Father's reaction is when one of His children is baptized with the Holy Spirit. What do you think the Father would say or do when *you* are baptized with the Holy Spirit?

I believe that there is nothing that could please God more than when a sinner repents and turn to Jesus (Luke 10:20; 2 Peter 3:9).

God loved and agreed with us before, but when we allow the Holy Spirit to direct and guide our lives, God is pleased. God knows that the believer's life will be lived much better when the Holy Spirit is manifesting Himself in their lives. Let's look at Jesus' first miracle after He was baptized with the Holy Spirit. Look at John:

> And the third day there was a marriage in Cana of Galilee; and the mother of Jesus was there: And both Jesus was called, and his disciples, to the marriage. And when they wanted wine, the mother of Jesus saith unto him, They have no wine. Jesus saith unto her, Woman, what have I to do with thee? mine hour is not yet come. His mother saith unto the servants, Whatsoever he saith unto you, do it. And there were set there six waterpots of stone, after the manner of the purifying of the Jews, containing two or three firkins apiece. Jesus saith unto them, Fill the waterpots with water. And they filled them up to the brim. And he saith unto them, Draw out now, and bear unto the governor of the feast. And they bare it. When the ruler of the feast had tasted the water that was made wine, and knew not whence it was: (but the servants which drew the water knew;) the governor of the feast called the bridegroom, And saith unto him, Every man at the beginning doth set forth good wine; and when men have well drunk, then that which is worse: but thou hast kept the good wine until now. This beginning of miracles did Jesus

in Cana of Galilee, and manifested forth his glory; and his disciples believed on him (John 2:1-11).

There is a lot to consider from the passage of Scripture above. However, the main thing I want to bring attention to is the productive power of Jesus through the Father. Remember what Jesus said:

> Then answered Jesus and said unto them, Verily, verily, I say unto you, The Son can do nothing of himself, but what he seeth the Father do: for what things soever he doeth, these also doeth the Son likewise (John 5:19).

The sole reason for the Holy Spirit is to create power in our lives— a supernatural power. Someone might ask, "Could Jesus have performed a miracle like this before being baptized with the Holy Spirit?" I suppose so if the Father instructed Him to. But there isn't a single recorded miracle in the Bible that He did before turning water into wine.

Three things happened because of the Presence and Power that Jesus displayed that day: Firstly, the needs of the people at the wedding were met. They wanted wine (John 2:3). I heard a man say, "God doesn't give us what we want, but only what we need." Well, I beg to differ. Jesus gave them what they wanted, not what they needed. In fact, the Bible does say:

> But my God shall supply all your need according to his riches in glory by Christ Jesus (Philippians 4:19).

The Kings James Translation uses the word "need," which indicates that we only have one need, and that need is Jesus. Look at this translation:

And my God will fulfill all your needs through His riches in glory in Christ Jesus (Philippians 4:19, Revised Geneva Translation).

This translation uses the word "needs." It's in the plural form, denoting that we have one or more needs. This is true. However, our only real need in life is, indeed, Jesus. But, just like the Scriptures above tell us, "all" our needs are fulfilled through God's riches if we are in Christ Jesus. The point is that when we are baptized with the Holy Spirit and His creative power is working within us and through us, not only are our needs met, but we are used to meeting the needs of others. Our need is met, and He fulfills the needs of others through the power working in us.

The second thing that happened because of the Holy Spirit's Presence and Power at the wedding is that the glory of Christ was revealed (John 2:11). Likewise, it's the same for believers who are baptized with the Holy Spirit. After we are baptized with the Holy Spirit, the glory of God should be seen in what we do, what we say, and where we go. Jesus was able to reveal His glory simply because He was called to the wedding (John 2:2). If Jesus wasn't called to the wedding, He wouldn't have had the opportunity to make known the glory of God through the Holy Spirit. There is no difference when it comes to us and the Holy Spirit. When we invite or call upon the Holy Spirit for help, we give Him the green light to reveal the glory of the Father through us. Remember, if we don't have a relationship with the Holy Spirit, we cannot expect to have fellowship with Him.

We already talked about water being a "type" of the Holy Spirit. But the Scripture also talks about rivers of living water flowing from our bellies when we put our trust in Him

(John 7:38). The term "rivers of living water" refers to the Spirit living inside us at the time of the new birth. It's important to note that John wasn't talking about the Holy Spirit because He hadn't come yet (v.39). When He came, that's when signs and wonders were revealed (Romans 15:19). Because I have rivers of living water flowing through me, I don't ever have to worry about getting thirsty again. Take a look at John again:

> Art thou greater than our father Jacob, which gave us the well, and drank thereof himself, and his children, and his cattle? Jesus answered and said unto her, Whosoever drinketh of this water shall thirst again: But whosoever drinketh of the water that I shall give him shall never thirst; but the water that I shall give him shall be in him a well of water springing up into everlasting life (John 4:12-14).

The verses above explain a lot about the Holy Spirit living inside of us. Jesus isn't talking about a physical thirst but a spiritual one. Jesus said the water which He gives would be in us forever and would flow through us for life. This water that Jesus is speaking of is the Holy Spirit.

Imagine you are doing yard work on a very sunny and hot day. You know it's important to stay hydrated, so you grab a bottle of cold water and drink it down. You can feel almost immediate relief from your thirst. You find the strength to continue working in the extreme heat of the day. After some time, you again feel the need to drink a bottle of water. Drinking water would probably continue throughout the day as long as you're out working in the yard. Whereas we have to appease our physical thirst consistently, Jesus tells us that after a believer is baptized with the Holy Spirit, he will no longer thirst for the things of the Spirit but instead stay satisfied and filled.

The third and last thing that happened because of the Holy Spirit's Presence and Power at the wedding is that the onlookers in attendance became stronger in their faith. When those that were present at the wedding saw what happened, they believed in Him (John 2:11). We know that the twelve disciples were present (John 2:2), but there were others present that were followers of Christ. Remember, this is a wedding. So, we can assume that there were family members there from both sides of the bride and groom and probably some very high governmental officials. I'm sure there were friends and people from the neighborhood attending the wedding, too. I believe more than just The Twelve witnessed what happened.

This is the Holy Spirit manifesting Himself through signs and wonders. This is what happens in your life and my life when we allow the Holy Spirit to have a free course in our life. He'll give us what we want, and as long as it doesn't go against His Word, He will show the glory of the Father in our life, increase our faith, and increase the faith of those around us.

Story #3: A Lame Man's Miracle

Let's look at another example of the Presence and Power of the Holy Spirit from Acts 3. This story is about a man being healed of a physical medical condition that he was born with. Let's pick up the story here:

Now Peter and John went up together into the temple at the hour of prayer, being the ninth hour. And a certain man lame from his mother's womb was carried, whom they laid daily at the gate of the temple, which is called Beautiful, to ask alms of them that entered into the temple; Who seeing Peter and John about to go into the temple asked an alms. And Peter, fastening his eyes upon him with John, said, Look on us. And he gave heed unto them, expecting to receive something of them. Then Peter said, Silver and gold have I none; but such as I have give I thee: In the name of Jesus Christ of Nazareth rise up and walk (Acts 3:1-6).

Every time I read this story, several questions go through my mind. Let's talk about a few of them. When Peter and John met his man, he was in one condition – bad. By the time they left him, he was in a much better condition—he was healed of his lifelong condition. Before we go any further, I want you to understand that regardless of your situation, the fact that you are reading this is evidence that things can change for the better.

The first question I have is: What is this man's problem? Let me explain. I know that he's lame and can't walk and has been in that condition since birth. I understand this because that's what the Scripture says. But I have a hard time understanding why he had been in that condition for so long. We know that he's at least 18 years old because the Bible says he's a man. We also know that someone brought him to the temple's gate every day at the same time. So, my first question is: why hasn't he experienced the Presence of the Holy Spirit until now?

Someone might say, "But the Holy Spirit had just made His presence known a few hours ago. Even Peter and John are new to Him." You're correct, but we've also already established that the Holy Spirit has been in operation since the Old Testament. The Holy Spirit didn't *live* in people of the Old Testament but rather came upon them. This man was asking for alms at the temple's gate every day, yet no one was able to offer him what he truly needed— healing. You would think that there was at least one priest or prophet visiting the temple for prayer that God could use to heal this man. It's not like he wasn't ready to be healed because he immediately responded to Peter when he said, "In the name of Jesus Christ of Nazareth, rise up and walk." So, what was this man's problem?

Could it be that he had never heard about the Holy Spirit? Or could it be that he had never been in the Presence of the Holy Spirit? Or maybe he was never introduced to the Holy Spirit? Whatever the reason, he stayed in that condition from the time of his birth up until the time he met Peter and John. When Peter told the man these words, "In the name of Jesus Christ of Nazareth, rise up and walk," what he did was invite the Presence of the Holy Spirit to show up.

However, right before he said those words, he qualified them with this phrase, "but such as I have give I thee." Peter recognizes the Holy Spirit living inside of him. This is Peter's way of communicating and fellowshipping with the Holy Spirit. Now that Peter had spoken, the Holy Spirit was given the green light to go to work. Peter's words alone were enough for the Holy Spirit to make His Presence amongst them. Remember, Peter and John were in the Upper Room when the Holy Spirit filled the house and the people in it, including them. Jesus taught them this truth:

> For verily I say unto you, That whosoever shall say unto this mountain, Be thou removed, and be thou cast into the sea; and shall not doubt in his heart, but shall believe that those things which he saith shall come to pass; he shall have whatsoever he saith. Therefore I say unto you, What things soever ye desire, when ye pray, believe that ye receive them, and ye shall have them (Mark 11:23-24).

Peter and John didn't have silver or gold to give him. Little did the man know that silver and gold weren't what he needed. He needed a touch from God. He needed to be in the Presence of the Holy Spirit. Peter and John were carrying out the commission that Jesus had left with them, which was to go into all the world and preach the gospel (Mark 16:15).

Peter and John were on fire for God. If you recall, in Acts 2, they were filled with the Holy Spirit, and right after the infilling, Peter preached a message, and about 3,000 people came to the Lord (Acts 2:41). Peter and John's encounter with this man was probably the same day, at three o'clock in the afternoon (Acts 3:1). Most likely, they had been praying in the Holy Spirit all day and were looking for someone to minister to. They knew that people would be at the temple for prayer during that time. They found a man at the gate they knew needed the Presence of the Holy Spirit for his situation. The Holy Spirit showed up in this man's life after years of living in a seriously debilitating state and depending on others daily. So, my first question remains: Why hadn't this man experienced the Presence and Power of the Holy Spirit before that day? I have a few possible reasons.

The Wrong Place

Even though the Holy Spirit lives inside us, if we don't acknowledge, communicate, or fellowship with Him, He will remain inactive in our lives. That's why Jude tells us to build ourselves up by praying in the Holy Spirit (Jude 20, New English Translation). Without the Holy Spirit's Presence and working Power in a believer's life, it can lead to being spiritually in the wrong place. This man was at church, but not in the church (Acts 2:2) I'm not suggesting that you will automatically experience the Power of the Holy Spirit if you are inside a church building and seated at your favorite seat. People can be inside the church and go through all the religious steps but have never heard of such a thing as the Holy Ghost. You and I can be somewhere that we think is the right place, but it's the wrong place for us. Being in the wrong place is one thing, but not even knowing that there's more for the believer after receiving the new birth is another thing. Look at the following verses:

> He said unto them, Have ye received the Holy Ghost since ye believed? And they said unto him, We have not so much as heard whether there be any Holy Ghost (Acts 19:2).

Sometimes, we can be in His Presence but never experience His Power. I think Jesus said it best when He went back to His hometown and was teaching in the synagogue. He said He couldn't perform many mighty works there because they didn't believe (Matthew 13:58).

You also don't have to be inside a church to experience the Presence or Power of the Holy Spirit. Our goal is to get into His Presence. We know that in the Presence of the Lord, there is fullness of joy (Psalm 16:11). So, I believe the environment has to be right for His Presence to show up. Peter and John were walking in the Presence of the Holy Spirit and operating under His power. Peter and John brought the Presence of the Holy Spirit into this man's life. So again, I ask, "How long would this man be carried to and from the gate if Peter and John hadn't shown up?"

After this man got into the Presence of the Holy Spirit, he received the Power of the Holy Spirit. We know from Scripture that this man only made it to the gate. I wonder, if someone had placed him inside the temple before Peter and John showed up, would he have experienced the Presence and Power of the Holy Spirit sooner? This further proves my point about how you don't have to be inside the church building to experience it. This man got his healing because two people baptized with the Holy Spirit were bold enough to go where no other man had gone—to the heart of this man's problem. He needed a touch of the Presence and Power of the Holy Spirit. The most important thing is that he was healed.

Spiritually Handicapped

Being ignorant or rejecting the Holy Spirit's place in our lives could cause one to become spiritually lame or spiritually dead. Jesus even warned us that people without the Holy Spirit operating in their lives can be physically well and living, but spiritually sick and dead. Look at Matthew:

> And another of his disciples said unto him, Lord, suffer me first to go and bury my father. But Jesus said unto him, Follow me; and let the dead bury their

dead. And when he was entered into a ship, his disciples followed him (Matthew 8:21-23).

Because of the changes that take place in a believer's life after he is baptized with the Holy Spirit, the absence of His involvement can be spiritually handicapping. I use the word "handicapping" because, without the Presence and Power of the Holy Spirit working in our lives, we're at a disadvantage. It restricts the blessings and promises we are entitled to. So, there are shortcomings and limitations that a believer lives with as a result.

According to the *Oxford English Dictionary*, the word "handicap" means something that makes it difficult for somebody to do something. This definition says a lot about the word "handicap." We know that this man was physically handicapped, but I submit to you that he was also spiritually handicapped. When believers aren't walking in the fullness of God, they're handicapped from receiving His intended blessings for them.

When the baptism of the Holy Spirit is missing from a believer's life, it can lead to shortcomings and limitations. Not that the spirit that God breathed inside us is flawed in any way because it's not. It just means without the Presence and Power of the Holy Spirit being active in a believer's life; they aren't operating at full capacity. Our lives aren't producing all that God intended. God knew this and gave us His Holy Spirit as a gift to close the void He knew His children would have as they lived for Him.

This man at the temple's gate was not only disabled to where his movement was impaired, but he also wasn't in the know. Because of his weakness of spirit, he wasn't going anywhere spiritually. This man was satisfied with just being at the gate. The reason I say he was satisfied is because he did the same thing, at the same place, at the same time, every day (Acts 3:2). This was a daily duty for this man. He had become satisfied with being carried by others to the temple's gate every day.

Please understand that I'm not making light of his condition at all. But, if we are satisfied with what others are doing for us, instead of trying to do for ourselves, then we'll remain spiritually handicapped. We won't be able to go anywhere without their help and assistance. He didn't even know how to receive his healing. Believers must live with the Holy Spirit being present and operating in their lives. In the natural sense, when we don't know what to do or how to do it, that's when we allow the Holy Spirit to take supernatural control. This man didn't know about the Holy Spirit. If he had, why was he looking for alms instead of something supernatural? (Acts 3:1).

This man needed a word of Power. Many times, we as Christians, spend too much time focusing on what people want instead of what they need. Peter and John didn't give this man what he wanted or was expecting to get, but they gave him what he needed. They didn't focus on what he was seeking. They knew that if he got what he wanted, which was money, he would be at the temple's gate the next day and all the days to follow. This man needed supernatural Power from the Holy Spirit.

When Peter and John looked at this man's condition, they quickly discerned that he didn't need material things like silver or gold, but rather, a word of Power. They knew that only a touch from God would supply what they needed. When believers who are baptized with the Holy Spirit look at people who are in need, what are we focused on? Most of the time, we as Christians, are looking at the outer condition of man and forget about the inner condition. If you get the inner man right, the outer man will come into alignment. What Peter and John gave this man was an inner Power that manifested Himself on the outside. All Peter and John had to do was change where this man was looking, and his whole view of life changed.

Sometimes all a person needs is to be in the Presence of the Holy Spirit, so that they can experience His supernatural Power. In the last three years, this is something I try to remember when I'm confronted with people who are in need. At present, I might not have anything material to offer them, but what I do have is the Holy Spirit living inside me that's waiting for me to give Him assignments. He is there not only to aid and assist us but also for us to be witnesses to others (Acts 1:8). The Holy Spirit can bring peace amidst conflict and joy in sad situations. When the Holy Spirit is present, there's a power to heal, deliver, and set free.

Story #4: The Presence and Power was in the Pool.

There is a story in the book of John that is, in many ways, like the one in Acts 3. In John 5, we find a man at a pool waiting for his healing:

> After this there was a feast of the Jews; and Jesus went up to Jerusalem. Now there is at Jerusalem by the sheep market a pool, which is called in the Hebrew tongue Bethesda, having five porches. In these lay a great multitude of impotent folk, of blind, halt, withered, waiting for the moving of the water.

For an angel went down at a certain season into the pool, and troubled the water: whosoever then first after the troubling of the water stepped in was made whole of whatsoever disease he had. And a certain man was there, which had an infirmity thirty and eight years. When Jesus saw him lie, and knew that he had been now a long time in that case, he saith unto him, Wilt thou be made whole? The impotent man answered him, Sir, I have no man, when the water is troubled, to put me into the pool: but while I am coming, another steppeth down before me. Jesus saith unto him, Rise, take up thy bed, and walk. And immediately the man was made whole, and took up his bed, and walked: and on the same day was the sabbath (John 5:1-9).

In the pool, there was a Power to heal the sick man. Unlike the story of the lame man, who was the only one at the gate of the temple, the man at the pool in this story was surrounded by other people who also needed healing. The man at the pool is, in a way, competing with others to be the first to get into the pool after it's troubled or stirred by the angel. All the impotent people at the pool came there to get into the Presence of the Holy Spirit, but more importantly, to experience His Power to receive their healing.

In the pool was a Power to heal their infirmity. Here is the word "infirmity" mentioned again. Remember, that means the inability to get results. This man had no ability to get results on his own. The Scripture doesn't reveal exactly what this man was suffering from, but it indicates that he was lame and possibly had no arms since he had some problems getting into the pool when the healing power was present. Whatever his condition was, it was incurable because he had been that way for 38 long years.

In my mind, this story presents lots of questions. If this man knew the season when the angel troubled the water, why wouldn't he position himself in an area by the pool that would make it easier to throw himself in? Whether the season was weekly, monthly, or yearly, this man was at the pool at the right time, hoping to get into the water when the angel troubled it. Furthermore, if he had suffered from his condition for 38 years, how long had he been lying at the pool waiting for someone to throw him in? One would think that if he couldn't walk to get into the pool, he could at least use his arms to help himself. Or maybe, he could have someone there to throw him in when the angel troubled the water. Regardless, he was there when he needed to be.

In both stories, these men, the lame one at the Gate Beautiful and the sick one at the pool of Bethesda, each received his healing by getting into the Presence of the Holy Spirit and experiencing the Power of the Holy Spirit. We need to understand that if we are going to be all that God intended for us to be, we must get into a place spiritually. If we aren't in a place spiritually, then we aren't in the right place. You could say that we are spiritually out of place. These men were spiritually out of place. One was at the church gate but not in church. The other man was close to the pool but never in the pool. When we get into church, the church gets in us, and when the church gets in us, that's when change takes place. Some so-called Christians are always at church, but the church never seems to be in them. I believe this is the reason Jesus instructed the disciples to remain in the Upper Room until they were endowed with the Holy Spirit.

Being spiritually out of place can cause a believer to miss out on the Promise of the Holy Spirit. The Bible says that there were about 120 believers who had received the instruction to remain in Jerusalem for the promise of the Holy Spirit. Look at Acts again:

> And, being assembled together with them, commanded them that they should not depart from Jerusalem, but wait for the promise of the Father, which, saith he, ye have heard of me. For John truly baptized with water; but ye shall be baptized with the Holy Ghost not many days hence. When they therefore were come together, they asked of him, saying, Lord, wilt thou at this time restore again the kingdom to Israel? And he said unto them, It is not for you to know the times or the seasons, which the Father hath put in his own power. But ye shall receive power, after that the Holy Ghost is come upon you: and ye shall be witnesses unto me both in Jerusalem, and in all Judaea, and in Samaria, and unto the uttermost part of the earth. And when he had spoken these things, while they beheld, he was taken up; and a cloud received him out of their sight. And while they looked steadfastly toward heaven as he went up, behold, two men stood by them in white apparel; Which also said, Ye men of Galilee, why stand ye gazing up into heaven? this same Jesus, which is taken up from you into heaven, shall so come in like manner as ye have seen him go into heaven. Then returned they unto Jerusalem from the mount called Olivet, which is from Jerusalem a sabbath day's journey. And when they were come in, they went up into an Upper Room, where abode both

Peter, and James, and John, and Andrew, Philip, and Thomas, Bartholomew, and Matthew, James the son of Alphaeus, and Simon Zelotes, and Judas the brother of James. These all continued with one accord in prayer and supplication, with the women, and Mary the mother of Jesus, and with his brethren. And in those days Peter stood up in the midst of the disciples, and said, (the number of names together were about a hundred and twenty) (Acts 1:4:15).

We've already talked about how Jesus' disciples and the others were obedient to stay in the Upper Room as Jesus instructed them. Because they did exactly what Jesus told them to do, they were spiritually in the right place. If any one of them had chosen to be in another place, he would have been spiritually out of place.

It takes unity for a group of people to stay together for a common cause. Inside the church is where togetherness and unity should be found. When the people of the church are found to be unified and have one common goal, the Holy Spirit is free to make known His Presence and Power.

People, even Christians, sometimes find themselves doing the same things over and over or going to the same place time and time again, and not even knowing why. I once heard someone say, "Sometimes, we stay in hell because we know the names of the streets." Sometimes people, including Christians, remain in the same place because they're familiar with or have very close associations with their surroundings. Sometimes, we can get too cozy with the routines of our life, which can keep us from what God has intended for us.

Both men that we read about knew how to get to the place where they were accustomed to going. They knew no other course of action to obtain their healing. They became comfortable with the very things that keep them from the Presence and Power of the Holy Spirit. They were okay with going to the place that they were accustomed to going to every day. One man found it more important just to get to the gate of the temple, rather than bother with getting inside the temple, while the other became comfortable with just being at the pool and not in the pool. Both had developed a spirit of complacency. I don't know about you, but I sure don't want to get comfortable in a place where the Holy Spirit isn't present and in operation.

When Brenda and I first returned to the United States and were searching for a home church, we visited several churches where we knew we were out of place. There was no excitement amongst the people nor from the pulpit. Every time this happened, I knew we had to keep searching for that one church that exemplified what we were finding in the Bible. We kept searching until we found the church that was surely the one for us. The Spirit of God was there, the power of God was there, and we felt right at home. 26 years later, we're still in that place. We know that where we are is the place that God called us to be. We're in our spiritual place. We're in a place where the Holy Spirit is present and has a free course to demonstrate His power with miracles, signs, and wonders.

Story #5: The Power of Discernment

I believe when believers are not baptized with the Holy Spirit with the evidence of speaking in other tongues, something is missing in their walk with Christ, which can be noticeable to other believers who are filled with the Holy Spirit. We already looked at this verse in Acts, but let's look a little deeper:

> And it came to pass, that, while Apollos was at Corinth, Paul having passed through the upper coasts came to Ephesus: and finding certain disciples, He said unto them, Have ye received the Holy Ghost since ye believed? And they said unto him, We have not so much as heard whether there be any Holy Ghost. And he said unto them, Unto what then were ye baptized? And they said, Unto John's baptism. Then said Paul, John verily baptized with the baptism of repentance, saying unto the people, that they should believe on him which should come after him, that is, on Christ Jesus. When they heard this, they were baptized in the name of the Lord Jesus. And when Paul had laid his hands upon them, the Holy Ghost came on them; and they spake with tongues, and prophesied. And all the men were about twelve (Acts 19:1-7).

Paul confronted twelve men that stood out to him who were either disciples of Jesus or believers that had not been baptized with the Holy Spirit. What was it about these men that got Paul's attention? Was it what they were saying? Was it how they were acting? Or was it something else? The Bible doesn't tell us why Paul asked the question: "Have ye received the Holy Ghost since ye believed?"

I personally believe that these twelve men were Jews who were in Jerusalem years before and had heard the preaching of John the Baptist and then received his water baptism for salvation. They believed in the coming Christ, whom John had proclaimed, but it appears that until this time, they hadn't received any more instruction in Christianity. Paul, perceiving this, asked them if they had received the Holy Ghost since they believed. At this point, the reason isn't important, but Paul decerned that there was something spiritually different about these men and himself.

Paul uses the term "certain disciples," which would indicate that they were known as disciples simply because they had repented of their sins and were water baptized to signify an outward cleansing. Paul also uses the phrase "since ye believed." He is clearly referring to a belief in Christ and not in John. These men had heard about the Holy Ghost from John the Baptist because he spoke of Him when he announced Christ's baptism with the Holy Ghost (Matthew 3:11; Luke 3:16), but they had not received the gospel of Christ. Therefore, these twelve men had not heard that there were extra, special gifts and powers of the Holy Spirit to be given to and received by anyone who believed in Christ.

So, we see that there is at least one place in the Bible where so-called believers didn't know anything about being baptized with the Holy Spirit to receive these extra, special gifts. I'm convinced that if we look throughout the body of Christ, we will discover many others.

In the stories we looked at, both men were at a disadvantage about how to receive their healing. The man at the Gate Beautiful had given up on being healed because he looked for alms each day. That's a bad place to find ourselves, giving up on what Jesus has already done for us and settling for something material. The man at the pool seems to be making an excuse for why he can't receive his healing. Jesus asked him an open-ended question: "Wilt thou be made whole?" Instead of answering Jesus with a "Yes," he instead chose to make an excuse about not having anyone to put him into the pool (John 5:6-7).

Notice how Jesus responded to the man's excuse: "Jesus saith unto him, Rise, take up thy bed, and walk" John 5:8). Jesus was operating in the Power of the Holy Spirit. Jesus Himself was the Presence of the Holy Spirit in that moment, and when He spoke the words, "Rise, take up thy bed, and walk," that was all the Holy Spirit needed to hear to respond to what Jesus had proclaimed with His mouth. Those words produced the Power needed to heal this man. Baptism with the Holy Spirit works the same way in a believer's life. We say what we want or need, and with the help of the Holy Spirit, there's a supernatural Power that comes to life inside us that produces results.

Sometimes, we tend to ignore spiritual things and reach for material things. I'll admit that material things may be easier to obtain at times. Therefore, I believe every believer needs to be baptized with the Holy Spirit. Both men were limited to the one method of healing known to them—the very thing that had gotten them to where they currently were—and so, they had become content with their way of living. Neither one of these men had experienced the Presence and Power of the Holy Spirit. Therefore, if you are baptized with the Holy Spirit or will be, I hope the next time you have an opportunity to witness to someone, you remember this, and lean on your inner power for help.

Story #6: A Visitation and Revelation

I want to share another personal story that I believe was the Holy Spirit operating supernaturally in my life. Other than sharing this story with Brenda and my sisters, as far as I can remember, this is my first time sharing this story publicly. There's no question in my mind that it was the Presence and the Power of the Holy Spirit doing one of the things He does best—bringing comfort. I was baptized with the Holy Spirit in 1996 while stationed in Okinawa, Japan. It wasn't until then that I started to witness supernatural things take place in my life. I will expound more on this later in the book. This story is just one of many supernatural experiences I've had where the Holy Spirit made Himself visible with power. This is just one of the examples of His miracles, signs, and wonders.

This supernatural event happened in 1996, during the same time I had come home from Okinawa, Japan, for my mother's funeral. My mother was a loving, God-fearing woman. She loved reading her Bible, praying, and attending church. Her unexpected passing was a shock to all that knew her. I used to call her every weekend from Okinawa, Japan. I can recall the day and time like it was yesterday when I got that phone call from one of my sisters. I remember going upstairs and lying across our bed and crying my eyes out. For the first five days, I really had a hard time with her departing. I'm careful not to use the word "death" here. I heard my pastor say that Christians don't die, they depart. So, I'll use "depart" or "passing" when speaking about her. I just couldn't understand how something like this could happen to my mother. You must understand that I had just rededicated my life back to Jesus two years before, I was new to the Holy Spirit, and I hadn't learned what the Bible says about the departed in Christ.

After waiting days to get a flight back to the United States, I tried my best to make sense of her passing. Finally, we made it to our destination. The day of the funeral came, and I was still, as some would say, "a hot mess." I knew I had to get myself together and act as if I was strong. At the funeral, I was able to speak a few words over my mother and hold it together, but I was broken inside. My heart was hurting! I think the main reason I was so hurt was that it was Thursday when I got the phone call about her departing, and I was scheduled to call her in two days. I didn't get a chance to hear her voice or see her, and I was hundreds of miles away from her. The fourteen-hour plane ride with all the connecting flights from Okinawa, Japan, to Memphis, Tennessee, seemed like it took forever.

After the funeral service and burial, for the rest of the day, I struggled to understand my mother's departing. I just could not accept the fact that she was gone and wasn't coming back. At some point, I began to sense that I was being too hard on myself and tried to find inner peace with the whole ordeal, but there was no peace to be found. So I thought, at least. I was just looking for peace in the wrong place.

After the funeral, Brenda and I spent the night with my youngest sister. I was still suffering from jetlag after my flight from Okinawa and had trouble falling asleep. All I could do was just lay there and think about my mother. I knew she was in Heaven, but my problem was not seeing or talking with her again. Once I finally fell asleep that night, something supernatural happened to me. What happened changed my whole perspective on how I viewed my mother's passing.

I'm not sure what time it was, but it was still dark outside, and everyone else in the house was asleep. As I was lying in bed, I'll say I was asleep, but I really can't be sure. I was taken to a place where I saw things that I had never seen before. It reminded me of the Scripture that talks about how eyes haven't seen, and ears haven't heard what God has in store for those who love Him (1 Corinthians 2:9). I didn't doubt that God loved my mother or me, but I wasn't expecting for Him to reveal a little of Heaven to me.

In my "sleep," God took me to a place that I'll call Heaven. I call it Heaven based on what I saw and the description in Revelation 21. Everything was so shiny and bright. I know that Revelation 21:1 says, "....and there was no more sea," but I saw a small body of water that was clear and blue as the sky. However, in Revelation 22:1, it says,

> And he shewed me a pure river of water of life, clear as crystal, proceeding out of the throne of God and of the Lamb.

I liken it to the "still waters" found in Psalms 23:2. The grass there was as green as it could get. The whole place was perfect and peaceful. I could've stayed and not returned to my sleep, but I knew that I was taken there for a reason. I sensed that my whole purpose for being there was to look for my mother.

As I began to look for her, flying from one room to another, there was no resistance in my ability to go through the walls of the many rooms that were in my path. I would go through one wall after another. As I was doing this, I kept looking for my mother. There were people all over the place, singing and laughing and just having a good time. This went on until I came to a body of water as I described above. When I saw the water, I fell from the air onto the green grass and started speaking in other tongues. At that moment, I woke up.

I lay there in bed wondering what that was all about. I woke up Brenda and asked her if she had heard me speaking in other tongues. She replied, "No," and didn't say anything else and went back to sleep. I got out of bed and kneeled next to the bed and asked God to reveal to me what He was trying to tell me. I got back into bed, closed my eyes, and immediately, I was back in that place repeating the same things—flying around through the walls and looking for my mother. And once again, I fell to the green grass and started to speak in other tongues. But this time, I don't remember waking back up until daylight the next morning.

I know this story is a bit lengthy, but I believe this was the Holy Spirit's way of comforting me amid my grief. Even though I never saw my mother, I knew in my spirit that she was at the place I dreamt about and that she was rejoicing along with the other saints there. The whole day following my Heavenly visit, and ever since then, I've had this incomprehensible peace concerning my mother's departure from this life. Like the Scripture says,

> And the peace of God, which passeth all understanding, shall keep your hearts and minds through Christ Jesus (Philippians 4:7).

Not only did I get a sense of peace, but also joy, which is beyond description since it entered my soul and to this day (1 Peter 1:8).

I didn't know that I could have such peace and joy at the passing of my mother or any other loved one. It's always God's will to give His children peace in all circumstances (2 Thessalonians 3:16). We don't have to live with irritation and conflict in our spirit about any area of our life.

Story #7: Walking with the Power of the Holy Spirit

For our next Presence and Power story of the Holy Spirit, we'll go to the book of Luke. It is the Holy Spirit that anoints us with His power. This story can also be found in Matthew and Mark. This wasn't Jesus' first time visiting Capernaum. Scripture would indicate that He attempted to keep His return quiet, but the news got out that He had returned (Mark 2:1, New Living Translation). Let's take a look at it:

> On one of those days, while he was teaching, Pharisees and teachers of the law were sitting there who had come from every village of Galilee and Judea, and also from Jerusalem. And the Lord's power to heal was in him (Luke 5:17, Christian Standard Bible).

There is a phrase from the above Scripture I want to focus on. The phrase is, "And the Lord's power to heal was in him." Notice that it says that Jesus had the Power of the Holy Spirit in Him to heal. Jesus just didn't come back to Capernaum as a special occasion to heal, He was there to preach the gospel. Neither did Jesus need to do anything special to possess the power to heal, He came there with the healing power in Him. The King James Version of the Bible says, "and the power of the Lord was present to heal them. The presence of the power was there because Jesus was there. My point is that Jesus showed up with the power in Him.

Likewise, when believers are filled with the Holy Spirit, wherever they go, they take the Power of the Holy Spirit in them. If we've been baptized with the Holy Spirit, we don't have to wait for Him to show up in a situation; He's living inside us and ready to go to work at our command. All we must do is invite Him by communicating with Him and telling Him what it is that we desire.

When Jesus gave the command, "thy sins are forgiven thee" (v.20), He was releasing the power that was in Him. That day, it was the power to heal because the Holy Spirit knew that there was at least one person that would show up that needed healing. When Jesus saw the need for healing, that was when He gave the command by the Holy Spirit to heal the man. It's no different for you or me. When we show up to a place where the Holy Spirit is present, there is an available power through Him to heal, deliver, set free, cast out demons, and save us.

It's just like when Jesus got word that His friend, Lazarus, had died. He commanded by the Power of the Holy Spirit that he come forth out of the grave (John 11:43-44). We've mentioned it before, but when Jesus came out of the wilderness and was confronted by the devil, He was able to defeat him because He had the Power of the Holy Spirit working in His life. Jesus was doing the works of the ministry of God (Luke 4:4). It was the same power operating in Jesus when He turned five loaves and two fish into a meal that fed over 5,000 people (Matthew 14:15-21). All these are miracles, signs, and wonders produced by the Power of the Holy Spirit.

Believers who are baptized with the Holy Spirit have that same power available to them, and He is ready to go to work on your behalf.

Chapter 3

Why Should Believers be Baptized with the Holy Spirit?

I hear this question asked quite often. So, I will try to answer it using Scriptural references. This is what I believe, so I'm ready to defend my belief. The church that I attended as a child and where I received my salvation didn't talk much about the Holy Spirit. As a matter of fact, if anything was said about Him, it wasn't about being baptized with Him. There was no mention of His Promise, Presence, or Power.

When He was referenced, He was always mentioned as the "Holy Ghost," but there was never talk about His supernatural power and speaking in other tongues because of being baptized with Him. If He was mentioned at all, it was from the reading of the Scripture. I've heard that some believe that the concept of "tongues" disappeared with the apostles. I don't believe this, and the Bible confirms it. Baptism with the Holy Spirit and speaking in other tongues are available for every believer in Christ, and He is real today.

Every time I'm asked the question, "Why should believers be baptized or filled with the Holy Spirit?" my answer is always the same: "He is a gift from the Father through His Son, Jesus, and is available to every believer who will ask for Him." Plus, there are personal reasons that I believe every believer should want to be baptized with the Holy Spirit with the evidence of speaking in other tongues. One is to allow God's supernatural power to operate in their life. Two, so that you can be a living witness to others about His power. Third, you get to experience and exercise boldness in witnessing. All three of these reasons are found throughout the Bible, but most importantly, right before Jesus went to Heaven to be with the Father, He left these words to the disciples and the church:

> But ye shall receive power, after that the Holy Ghost comes upon you: and ye shall be witnesses unto me both in Jerusalem, and in all Judaea, and in Samaria, and unto the uttermost part of the earth (Acts 1:8).

So, these are the reasons that every believer should desire to be baptized with the Holy Spirit.

Remember, baptism with the Holy Spirit is available to every believer (Acts 2:39), and the Bible encourages every believer to receive this gift (Acts 19:2, 1 Corinthians 14:18). The apostle Paul, who wrote over half of the New Testament, was baptized with the Holy Spirit and spoke in other tongues. Paul was a follower of Christ and instructed believers to follow his teaching as he follows the teaching of Christ. Paul said,

> You must follow my example, as I follow the example of Christ (1 Corinthians 11:1, Contemporary English Version).

From the translation above, Paul was firm on what he believed. He uses the word "must," which means following Christ shouldn't be something we neglect. Not to be redundant, but we have already seen that Jesus was baptized with the Holy Spirit, and it pleased the Father (Matthew 3:16-17). The greatest apostles of the New Testament were also baptized with the Holy Spirit and spoke in tongues. The Holy Spirit is a heavenly gift that lives in earthly vessels. He is no longer just with us but lives inside us (2 Corinthians 4:7). The Holy Spirit is a treasured gift given by the Father to His children. So, my question to you is: What's stopping you?

We Receive the God Kind of Love

When believers are filled or baptized with the Holy Spirit with the evidence of speaking in other tongues, they receive the same love that God loves us with. We already know that there's a supernatural power that's given to a believer when he is baptized with the Holy Spirit to do the work of the ministry and to be a witness of Christ all around the world (Acts 1:8). With this power, a believer can know and do things that they wouldn't otherwise be capable of knowing or doing. But the Bible also says the love of God has come to live in our hearts by the Holy Spirit (Romans 5:5). I want to look at this verse in Romans in its full context and from a different translation:

> Therefore, since we have been made right in God's sight by faith, we have peace[a] with God because of what Jesus Christ our Lord has done for us. Because of our faith, Christ has brought us into this place of undeserved privilege where we now stand, and we confidently and joyfully look forward to sharing God's glory. We can rejoice, too, when we run into problems and trials, for we know that they help us develop endurance. And endurance develops strength of character, and character strengthens our confident hope of salvation. And this hope will not lead to disappointment. For we know how dearly God loves us, because he has given us the Holy

Spirit to fill our hearts with his love (Romans 5:1-5, New Living Translation).

Because of what Jesus did on the cross, we're justified by our faith and, therefore, have been reconciled back to God and have peace with Him. What Satan meant for our failure and destruction was turned so that we can be made right with God by our faith in Jesus Christ. Therefore, because of our reconciliation with God, we can be joyful about the glory He has extended toward us. When we're faced with troubles in life, we have the hope and staying power to help us push on through. This hope that He gives is not a false hope but one that will surely succeed. I wanted to say all that before I could say this: All the peace, joy, endurance, and hope we have through our faith in Jesus Christ is all possible through the Father's love for us.

The same love that He loves us with, He has poured that love into our hearts by the Holy Spirit. The latter part of Romans 5:5 says, "Because he has given us the Holy Spirit to fill our hearts with his love." Notice it says, "with His love." When a believer is baptized with the Holy Spirit, his heart is filled with the love of God. Because God is love (1 John 4:8), and we are filled with the Holy Spirit, we can live by faith, have peace, be joyful, and persevere in hard times. This is all done through the works of the Holy Spirit.

So, other than the power, and all that comes with it, which the Holy Spirit gives, we can now see that He pours into our hearts the same love which He loves us with. It's no doubt that God loves humanity, and at the new birth, we experience His love for us. But this love I am speaking of, which is poured out in our hearts at the baptism of the Holy Spirit, is the same love He loves the world with and the same love He was willing to express to pay for my sins and yours (1 Corinthians 6:20). This is the same love that He was willing to show toward the world by the death of His Son, Jesus (John 3:16).

Could a lack of baptism with the Holy Spirit be the reason that many believers have problems doing the things the Bible says love should cause them to do? Look at Corinthians:

> Love does not give up. Love is kind. Love is not jealous. Love does not put itself up as being important. Love has no pride. Love does not do the wrong thing. Love never thinks of itself. Love does not get angry. Love does not remember the suffering that comes from being hurt by someone. Love is not happy with sin. Love is happy with the truth. Love takes everything that comes without giving up. Love believes all things. Love hopes for all things. Love keeps on in all things (1 Corinthians 13:4-7, New Life Version).

We're living in a time when the world could use more love. But Paul is speaking to the church at Corinth. He is preaching to believers of Christ and telling them that love is the foundation of how they should live. Just think for one minute, if all believers truly believed and practiced love the way it is presented here by Paul, wouldn't we have a better world to live in? I truly believe so. But you and I both know that many believers struggle with expressing their love in such a way. Could it be because they are not baptized with the Holy Spirit?

As a believer myself, I can tell you that it wasn't easy for me to express love toward others the way that Paul instructs believers to before I was baptized with the Holy Spirit. I believe that when Christians are baptized with the Holy Spirit, it enables them to express God's kind of love toward others in the same way that God has and is expressing His love toward us. The passage above about love is the way God wants His children to express their love toward one another. Because God is love, His love is given to us at the new birth. But in my opinion, to love at the level Paul is speaking about requires baptism with the Holy Spirit.

I know someone might ask, "Are you saying that believers can't love the way Paul described unless they are baptized with the Holy Spirit?" You would have to agree that the way Paul tells believers to love is a tall order to fill. If we are honest with ourselves, we would have to admit that this is something that we can't do on our own. It takes a higher power working within us, and that higher power is the Holy Spirit. We all know that from our viewpoint, sometimes people are unlovable. Even people who are close to us, like our family members, can be hard to love at times, whether it's because of their way of living or their negative behavior. I think believers and non-believers both have a sense of what it means to love someone. But when we are challenged to love others the way Christ loves us (believer or nonbeliever), we all fall short.

I can honestly say since I was baptized with the Holy Spirit, I have seen a change in my love for others. In the times we live in, I can't imagine trying to live my life to the standard of love presented here without the Holy Spirit's help. I believe that the same love that is poured out in our hearts by the Holy Spirit (Romans 5:5), is the same love that causes us to be able to do the things that love should cause us to do. Look what the Bible says in Galatians:

But the fruit of the Spirit is love, joy, peace, longsuffering, gentleness, goodness, faith, Meekness, temperance: against such there is no law (Galatians 5:22-23).

I'm not suggesting that a believer who isn't baptized with the Holy Spirit can't love and doesn't have joy, peace, longsuffering, gentleness, goodness, faith, meekness, or temperance. I'm sure that they can do these things, but up to a certain limit. I know from my own life that before I was baptized with the Holy Spirit with the evidence of speaking in other tongues, the fruit of the Spirit in my life was nearly nonexistent. I didn't even know that I could live my life in such a way. The fruit of the Spirit must be developed on purpose by operating in it. I thought it was based on my feelings or convenience. After my baptism with the Holy Spirit, I saw it as my duty to live with the fruit of the Spirit operating and visible in my life. It's a lifestyle, not just when I feel like it or when it's convenient.

The product of the Spirit is the love of God expressing Himself in believers through the works of the Holy Spirit. It is God's love given to us through the works of the Holy Spirit that enables believers who are baptized with the Holy Spirit to never give up, be kind, never be jealous, show no pride, always do the right thing, always think of others, be peaceful, always forgive, hate sins, embrace truth, believe the best about everyone, and always hope for the best. And if these are not enough reasons to desire being baptized with the Holy Spirit, according to 1 Corinthians 13:8, "Love never fails." Love always wins, so love is reason enough.

Chapter 4

Do Not Be Ignorant about Tongues

I know that I've been talking about speaking in other tongues a lot. You might ask, "How does one begin to speak in other tongues after being baptized with the Holy Spirit?" That's a good question. To tell you the truth, I don't know how all that works. All I know is that when I was baptized with or filled with the Holy Spirit, my lips began to tremble, and I started to make sounds that were unknown to me. The words and phrases coming from my mouth sounded like I was speaking in a foreign language. It was a foreign language because it was foreign to me. The only language I knew at the time, and even today, is English. This language did not come from me. The tongues just came upon me. I didn't create them, and nor did I try to stop them. They were as the Spirit gave me utterance (Acts 2:4). My job was to cooperate with what the Holy Spirit was doing just as the Father, the Son, and the Holy Spirit agree and collaborate to jointly produce miracles, signs, and wonders. Thank God that everyone in the room that morning was already baptized with the Holy Spirit with the evidence of speaking in other tongues. Otherwise, they would've thought something similar about me as the onlookers did in Acts 2 when they thought the believers were drunk as they first started speaking in other tongues.

I hope by now that you're ready to be baptized with the Holy Spirit and speak in other tongues. However, I feel the need to address one more thing: speaking in other tongues. Some of you might be saying, "I'm fine with the baptism of the Holy Spirit, but that speaking in other tongues thing is a little too much." Some of you might be thinking and feeling what I thought and felt when I first heard someone speak in other tongues. To tell you the truth, I didn't know what to think (1 Corinthians 14:23). My first thought was, "Why are they speaking that way? No one understands them. Is something wrong with them?" But there was one thing I did know. I knew that I wanted nothing to do with those people and their church.

This is what happens when we're ignorant of the Scripture (Matthew 22:29). Paul spoke about many things that believers shouldn't be ignorant about. One of them was speaking in an unknown tongue (1 Corinthians 12). Speaking in tongues is a spiritual gift that's offered to every believer who's been baptized with the Holy Spirit. Like I said before, other than the gift of salvation, the gift of the Holy Spirit is second to none. So, I understand what you might be thinking or feeling about speaking in other tongues. Let's see if we can change your mind. Look at 1 Corinthians:

> For he that speaketh in an unknown tongue speaketh not unto men, but unto God: for no man understandeth him; howbeit in the spirit he speaketh mysteries. But he that prophesieth speaketh unto men to edification, and exhortation, and comfort. He that speaketh in an unknown tongue edifieth himself; but he that prophesied edifieth the church. I would that ye all spake with tongues but rather that ye prophesied: for greater is he that prophesieth than he that speaketh with tongues, except he interpret, that the church may receive edifying. Now, brethren, if I

come unto you speaking with tongues, what shall I profit you, except I shall speak to you either by revelation, or by knowledge, or by prophesying, or by doctrine? And even things without life-giving sound, whether pipe or harp, except they give a distinction in the sounds, how shall it be known what is piped or harped? For if the trumpet give an uncertain sound, who shall prepare himself to the battle? So likewise ye, except ye utter by the tongue words easy to be understood, how shall it be known what is spoken? for ye shall speak into the air. There are, it may be, so many kinds of voices in the world, and none of them is without signification. Therefore if I know not the meaning of the voice, I shall be unto him that speaketh a barbarian, and he that speaketh shall be a barbarian unto me. Even so ye, forasmuch as ye are zealous of spiritual gifts, seek that ye may excel to the edifying of the church. Wherefore let him that speaketh in an unknown tongue pray that he may interpret. For if I pray in an unknown tongue, my spirit prayeth, but my understanding is unfruitful. What is it then? I will pray with the spirit, and I will pray with the understanding also: I will sing with the spirit, and I will sing with the understanding also. Else when thou shalt bless with the spirit, how shall he that occupieth the room of the unlearned say Amen at thy giving of thanks, seeing he understandeth not what thou sayest? For thou verily givest thanks well, but the other is not edified. I thank my God, I speak with tongues more than ye all: Yet, in the church, I had rather speak five words with my understanding, that by my voice I might teach others also, than ten thousand words in an unknown tongue (1 Corinthians 14:2-19).

That's a long passage of Scripture, but I thought it was necessary to help you understand the importance of speaking in other tongues. Notice that Paul tells us that when we speak in an unknown tongue, we speak unto God and not to man. This is one of the beauties of speaking in other tongues—the devil doesn't know what you're communicating to God. Yes, it's also true that we don't know what we're saying unless the Holy Spirit reveals it to us. But the most important thing is that we're praying according to the perfect will of God, just like we've already learned from Romans 8:26, which reads:

> Likewise the Spirit also helpeth our infirmities: for we know not what we should pray for as we ought: but the Spirit itself maketh intercession for us with groanings which cannot be uttered (Romans 8:26).

We also learned that Paul spoke in tongues more than other believers at the Corinth church to edify the church. But even though Paul understood the importance of speaking in other tongues, most importantly, he understood that it was important for people to understand his message. Therefore, he spoke in his native tongue just so the people could understand what he was saying. Paul chose to edify the church in his native language other than in other tongues. Speaking in tongues for edifying the church is as the Spirit wills. Not as we will. This isn't something we do on our own, but as the Holy Spirit moves within us.

Paul also understood the importance of speaking in other tongues for personal edification and did it willingly. I used the word "willing," because it was something that Paul did at his will. Paul teaches us that we can pray in other tongues, pray in our native tongue, sing in other tongues, and sing with understanding as we desire to (1 Corinthians 14:15). The point is, as believers baptized with the Holy Spirit with the evidence of speaking in other tongues, we can pray or sing in unknown tongues just as we can sing and pray in our native language whenever we desire to. This is a powerful weapon that God has made available to His children. What believer wouldn't want this weapon in his arsenal?

There's one more point I want to highlight from the passage of Scripture above; Speaking in other tongues as a believer is for personal use and a choice. It is not a commandment. I can't find anywhere in the Bible where Jesus or God commanded believers to speak in other tongues. Remember, Paul said to the church at Corinth that he wished that they all spoke in other tongues but preferred that they prophesied to edify the church (1 Corinthians 14:5). So, I'm not suggesting that speaking in other tongues is a requirement directed by the Bible, but what I am suggesting is that speaking in other tongues is a byproduct of being baptized with the Holy Spirit, which provides the believer with supernatural power to do and know things about God and Jesus that otherwise wouldn't be done or known.

Now that you have more knowledge on the subject, and even though it's not a commandment, why wouldn't you want this gift as a believer? When a believer is baptized with the Holy Spirit with the evidence of speaking in unknown tongues, the unknown tongues here are not used for church settings. Personal tongues are not for the edification of the church but rather for the edification of one's soul and spirit. This isn't to say that the Holy Spirit won't use you to speak in an unknown tongue to edify the church. If He does, then it's considered prophesying. Please don't misunderstand this. I believe many believers have confused individual prayer language (speaking in other tongues) with prophesying. One's individual prayer language can be interpreted by you (1 Corinthians 14:13), but it isn't for edifying the church or a group. Please read and study the entire chapter of 1 Corinthians 14 for a better understanding of speaking in other tongues.

The Bible also instructs believers to stay filled with the Holy Spirit. Look at Ephesians:

> Don't drink too much wine, for many evils lie along that path; be filled instead with the Holy Spirit and controlled by him (Ephesians 5:18, Living Bible).

Another reason to speak in other tongues after you are filled with the Holy Spirit is to be refilled or stay filled. As the cares of this world invade our lives, we can leak. The leaking of the Holy Spirit is caused by just living life. It's imperative that believers who have been baptized with the Holy Spirit stay filled with Him. When we stay filled with Him, we're controlled by Him just like a person filled with wine is controlled by wine. We must stay full of the Holy Spirit if we desire to live a Spirit-controlled life.

Jesus was full of the Holy Spirit when He was led into the wilderness (Luke 4:1) The Bible says that Stephen was full of faith and the Holy Spirit (Acts 6:5). There was also Barnabas, who was full of the Holy Spirit and strong in faith (Acts 11:24). You might ask, "How do I stay full of the Holy Spirit?" Just as we've already learned from Romans 8:26, when we pray in other tongues, the Spirit helps us understand and know the things that we need at the time.

Before we move forward, there is one more Scripture I want to share with you. It's found in Jude:

But you, dear friends, carefully build yourselves up in this most holy faith by praying in the Holy Spirit, staying right at the center of God's love, keeping your arms open and outstretched, ready for the mercy of our Master, Jesus Christ. This is the unending life, the real life! (Jude 20-21, Message Bible).

What a powerful passage from the Scriptures. We see that praying in the Holy Spirit, what's known as praying in other tongues, builds the believer up in his inner spirit. But most importantly, it keeps believers in the center of God's love. This is the life that every believer should strive for. Remember, it's by the Holy Spirit that God's love is placed in our hearts (Romans 5:5). With the flesh constantly trying to suppress believers from walking in the spirit, it's the love of God given by the Holy Spirit that helps believers love those who seems unlovable. Without the Holy Spirit, it would be impossible to love others the way that God loves us.

Believers who are baptized with the Holy Spirit with the evidence of speaking in other tongues can be filled and stay full of the Holy Spirit by using their prayer language to speak in other tongues. This is a powerful gift that God has left the church. In this crazy world, it's hard to understand how believers could function in everyday life without the Holy Spirit operating and controlling their life.

I hope by now you're asking, "How can I be baptized with the Holy Spirit with the evidence of speaking in other tongues?" I'm glad you asked. I've been patiently waiting for the opportunity to tell you how. It's easier than you might think. I first want to make you aware of the truth. That is, Jesus is the Baptizer or Filler of the Holy Spirit (Matthew 3:11). This is neither man's doing, nor can you receive the filling or baptism of the Holy Spirit from any university or seminary. But there is one prerequisite for being baptized with the Holy Spirit, which is, you must be a born-again believer (Romans 10: 9-10). Therefore, if you haven't asked Jesus into your heart, let's take care of that right now. Pray this prayer:

> Dear heavenly Father, I come to You as a sinner. Today, I am asking You to come and live in my heart. I repent of all my sins. I accept You today, Jesus. Thank You for giving me new life and a new nature. Satan, sin, I don't serve you anymore. From this day forward, I will serve You, Jesus Christ. I make Jesus Christ my Lord and Savior. Amen.

Congratulations! You are now part of the family of God. You might say, "That was easy!" You're right; God has made it that simple. We're the ones that make it hard. Now, I know you meant what you just prayed. So now you must tell someone what you just did. Telling someone is vitally important. Don't you think it's important to confess your salvation to someone? Look at Luke:

> Also, I say unto you, Whosoever shall confess me before men, him shall the Son of man also confess before the angels of God: But he that denieth me before men shall be denied before the angels of God (Luke 12:8-9).

Paul even said that he was not ashamed of the gospel of Jesus Christ (Romans 1:16-17). Also, it's equally as important for you to find a church where the Bible is taught and where the Spirit of God is free to move, for you to attend regularly, and for you to read your Bible. Your life is about to change for the better.

Being baptized with the Holy Spirit is just as easy as being born again. Paul talked about the simplicity of the gospel (2 Corinthians 11:3). Sometimes, we as believers try to read too much into the Scripture when it comes to being born again and baptized with the Holy Spirit. Let's look at Luke again to see just how easy it is:

> And I say unto you, Ask, and it shall be given you; seek, and ye shall find; knock, and it shall be opened unto you. For everyone that asketh receiveth; and he that seeketh findeth; and to him that knocketh it shall be opened. If a son shall ask bread of any of you that is a father, will he give him a stone? or if he ask a fish, will he for a fish give him a serpent? Or if he shall ask an egg, will he offer him a scorpion? If ye then, being evil, know how to give good gifts unto your children: how much more shall your heavenly Father give the Holy Spirit to them that ask him (Luke 11:9-13).

It's as simple as asking Him to baptize you with the Holy Spirit and then receive Him by faith. If you recall, in John 20, Jesus appeared to the disciples, and after talking with them, He breathed on them and told them to receive the Holy Ghost (John 20:22).

Baptism with the Holy Spirit is done by simply asking and receiving. There's no other way to receive this gift from the Father. Ben Patterson said this about Nathaniel Hawthorne: "He described happiness as a butterfly, which, when pursued, is always just beyond your grasp, but which, if you sit down quietly, may alight upon you. And it's like that with the Spirit of God. He is not seized. He is received." He isn't something we can reach out to and grab. He must be received. When we ask and believe, then we receive Him by faith. When a believer is baptized with the Holy Spirit with the evidence of speaking in other tongues, there is a new revelation available to him that he never had before. It's like this formula:

Revelation + Application = Elevation

I remember when I was baptized with the Holy Spirit, as if it just happened today. It was in 1995. I was on active duty at the time, stationed in Okinawa, Japan. It was a Sunday morning before service started. The pastor of the church, myself, and a few other leaders were gathered in the pastor's study to pray like we did every Sunday morning before service. I could sense that this Sunday morning was not like any other Sunday morning when we had joined together for prayer. I could sense the Spirit of the Lord was present in the room, and something supernatural was about to happen. As we continued to pray, one of the people in the room, who was an evangelist, laid her hand on my forehead and began to pray in other tongues. When she touched my forehead, I remember falling to the floor and hearing myself praying in other tongues. I was told that I was on the floor for some time before I was helped up.

You might be asking, "Why am I telling you this story?" Before that Sunday morning experience, I only had a hunger for the Word of God. But after being baptized with the Holy Spirit with the evidence of speaking in other tongues, I developed an appetite for the Word of God. I noticed myself desiring to read the Bible more and to know more about God. I found myself wanting to do those things that would be pleasing in God's eyes instead of doing those things that were pleasing to me. From that day until now, I've been proclaiming that it was God who gave me His Holy Spirit (1 Thessalonians 4:8). On that Sunday morning, I was blessed with the greatest blessing a human being could receive. Look at Matthew:

> Great blessings belong to those who want to do right more than anything else. God will fully satisfy them (Matthew 5:6, Easy-to-Read Version).

I wanted to do it right more than anything. Jesus met me at every challenge I faced and delivered me from its danger. I had the desire to do the greater works that Jesus spoke about after He was gone to the Father and the Holy Spirit became the one active Person in His life (John 14:12). What happened to me on that Sunday morning changed my life forever, for the better. The best way I can describe what happened to me is that the Holy Spirit that was already living inside me received a promotion from God to do the things in my life that I couldn't do on my own. That may not be the best illustration, but it's the best way I can explain what happened to me. Things started to happen in my life that I can't explain to this day why they turned out that way. But I give all the glory to my Lord and Savior, Jesus Christ.

With the baptism of the Holy Spirit came revelation. This wasn't just a one-time thing. It was a progressive revelation. Then, after I started to apply the revelations He gave me, I witnessed my personal life starting to elevate to a new level. I can tell you without apology that my life hasn't been the same since. After I was baptized with the Holy Spirit with the evidence of speaking in other tongues, I gained a new revelation about God and how much He loved me. This was something I had never experienced before. I knew He loved me because the Bible told me He did. But to have such a strong sense of His love for me was never there before. After I was filled with the Holy Spirit with the evidence of speaking in other tongues, every time I read the Bible, there was a satisfaction of knowing I was important to God and that He cares deeply about me. With these revelations, my hunger and thirst for Him grew more day by day. I have found that the more I seek Him, the more He reveals Himself to me.

Conclusion

I have shared with you some of my personal stories of the Holy Spirit operating in my life. Since I was baptized with the Holy Spirit, I have experienced His presence and power, and I must say, He has truly changed my life for the better.

For many years, I didn't know about the promise of the Holy Spirit. As a believer, I lived way below the plan and purpose God had for me. I knew there had to be more to life than what I was experiencing. I was constantly asking God to bless me. My blessings were sporadic. Then one day, I realized why my blessings were a hit-or-miss in my life. You see, even when I discovered the Promise of the Holy Spirit, I had never experienced the Presence or Power of the Holy Spirit.

I will use the words of the apostle Paul, "I beseech you.".

I beseech you to be baptized with the Holy Spirit with the evidence of speaking in other tongues if you haven't since you believed.

Made in the USA
Monee, IL
04 March 2025